11+ Verbal Reasoning
Vocabulary
For the CEM test

A good vocabulary is a must for success in the CEM 11+, so we've made a whole book of 10-Minute Tests to help boost children's word power.

Each test is packed with CEM-style practice at the perfect level for ages 10-11, all with detailed answers included. Nobody does 11+ prep better than CGP!

10-Minute Tests

Ages 10-11

How to access your free Online Edition

This book includes a free Online Edition to read on your PC, Mac or tablet.
You'll just need to go to **cgpbooks.co.uk/extras** and enter this code:

3355 2414 8197 5654

By the way, this code only works for one person. If somebody else has used this book before you, they might have already claimed the Online Edition.

How to use this book

This book is made up of 10-minute tests and puzzle pages.
There are answers at the back of the book.

10-Minute Tests

- There are 31 tests in this book, each containing 25 questions.

- Each test is designed to target the type of vocabulary questions that your child could come across in the verbal reasoning section of their 11+ test, and covers a variety of questions at the right difficulty level.

- Your child should aim to score at least 21 out of 25 in each of the 10-minute tests.
  If they score less than this, use their results to work out the areas they need more practice on.

- If your child hasn't managed to finish the test in time, they need to work on increasing their speed, whereas if they have made a lot of mistakes, they need to work more carefully.

- Keep track of your child's scores using the progress chart at the back of the book.

Puzzle Pages

- There are 12 puzzle pages in this book, which are a great break from test-style questions.
  They encourage children to practise the skills that they will need in the test, but in a fun way.

Published by CGP

Editors:
Chloe Anderson, Claire Boulter, Emma Cleasby, Sophie Herring, Katya Parkes

With thanks to Holly Robinson and Alison Griffin for the proofreading.

Please note that CGP is not associated with CEM in any way.
This book does not include any official questions and it is not endorsed by CEM.

ISBN: 978 1 78908 187 9
Printed by Elanders Ltd, Newcastle upon Tyne
Clipart from Corel®

Based on the classic CGP style created by Richard Parsons.

Text, design, layout and original illustrations © Coordination Group Publications Ltd. (CGP) 2018
All rights reserved.

Photocopying this book is not permitted, even if you have a CLA licence.
Extra copies are available from CGP with next day delivery. • 0800 1712 712 • www.cgpbooks.co.uk

Contents

Test 1 2
Test 2 5

Puzzles 1 7

Test 3 8
Test 4 11

Puzzles 2 14

Test 5 15
Test 6 18
Test 7 20

Puzzles 3 23

Test 8 24
Test 9 27
Test 10 30

Puzzles 4 32

Test 11 33
Test 12 36
Test 13 39

Puzzles 5 42

Test 14 43
Test 15 46
Test 16 49

Puzzles 6 52

Test 17 53

Test 18 55
Test 19 58

Puzzles 7 60

Test 20 61
Test 21 64
Test 22 67

Puzzles 8 70

Test 23 71
Test 24 74
Test 25 77

Puzzles 9 79

Test 26 80
Test 27 83

Puzzles 10 86

Test 28 87
Test 29 90

Puzzles 11 93

Test 30 94
Test 31 97

Puzzles 12 100

Answers 101

Progress Chart 124

Test 1

You have **10 minutes** to do this test. Work as quickly and as accurately as you can.

> Underline the correct homophone to complete the sentence.
>
> **Example**:   Archie tied a _____ in the ship's rigging.   not   <u>knot</u>

1. Rob planted a _____ tree.   ewe   yew
2. Isha _____ being at her old school.   mist   missed
3. There was a _____ smell in the air.   foul   fowl
4. Wild _____ eat an omnivorous diet.   boors   bores   boars
5. That was the best _____ in the play.   seen   scene
6. Don't _____ in other people's lives.   meddle   medal

> Find the word that is a synonym, or nearly a synonym, of the word on the left.
>
> **Example**:   **wide**   flat   straight   <u>broad</u>   long

7. **acquire**   obtain   allow   admit   discover
8. **threaten**   defeat   intimidate   impose   surprise
9. **unwelcome**   unavoidable   unacceptable   regrettable   undesirable
10. **dread**   apprehension   uncertainty   discomfort   irritation
11. **reinstate** summon   restore   uncover   redeem
12. **suitable**   pleasurable   satisfying   appropriate   innovative

Complete the word on the right so that it is an antonym, or nearly an antonym, of the word on the left.

Example: smooth r o u g h

13. implausible   c _ _ d i b _ e
14. gratify   _ i s _ l e _ s e
15. capability   _ _ a _ _ l i t y
16. withheld   g r _ n _ e _
17. expressive   _ n e m _ t _ _ n a _
18. disparage   p r _ _ s _

Choose the correct three-letter word to complete the word in capital letters, so that it finishes the sentence in a sensible way.

Example: It can be **CHY** outside when it snows.

  APP **ILL** EEK ERR

19. Brian tried to stop the boat from **SING**.

  INK LAY NOW EAT

20. Davood felt **REVED** that it was the summer holidays.

  PRO AMP CUR LIE

21. Oscar **SCED** his knee against the concrete.

    OWL   RIB   RAP   OFF

22. Five **CES** of apples were stacked in the cellar.

    HID   RAN   RAT   HIM

23. The **SCH** continues for the lost dog.

    EAR   TAR   WIT   COT

24. The teacher spent his evening **MING** the homework.

    ILK   ARK   ASK   END

25. The prince wanted to be **GRER** than his father.

    ASP   ATE   OUT   ANT

END OF TEST

/ 25

Test 2

You have **10 minutes** to do this test. Work as quickly and as accurately as you can.

> Three of the words in each list are linked. Mark the word that is not related to these three.
>
> **Example**:   teacher   doctor   <u>hospital</u>   firefighter

1. onerous   formidable   endurable   taxing
2. oversee   scrutinise   manage   supervise
3. ingenious   inventive   resourceful   haughty
4. rivet   engross   capture   preoccupy
5. actor   director   dancer   singer

> Find the word that is an antonym, or nearly an antonym, of the word on the left.
>
> **Example**:   **first**   later   <u>last</u>   next   beginning

6. **frail**   capable   puny   hearty   gleeful
7. **overbearing**   plucky   meek   reckless   diplomatic
8. **rude**   courteous   obliging   tender   aloof
9. **unity**   dissection   division   merger   displacement
10. **arrest**   disentangle   apprehend   extract   liberate

Select the most appropriate word from the table to complete each pair of synonyms below. Write the word on the corresponding line.

| develop | unique | warily | adequately | wane |
| venture | infirmity | veil | dedicated | charm |

11. lessen _____

12. zealous _____

13. decrepitude _____

14. formulate _____

15. gingerly _____

16. captivate _____

17. sufficiently _____

18. mask _____

19. singular _____

20. endeavour _____

Mark the word outside the brackets that has a similar meaning to the words in both sets of brackets.

Example: (find discover) (stain blemish)   freckle smudge <u>spot</u> see

21. (hem edging)   (perimeter boundary)   border line enclosure surround

22. (shred mince)   (scrape rasp)   pulverise mangle grate inflame

23. (accept enrol)   (confess concede)   admit entrance recruit bare

24. (attire outfit)   (consistent constant)   costume similar garb uniform

25. (place location) (meaning purpose)   intent essence point idea

END OF TEST

/ 25

Puzzles 1

Time for a break! These puzzles are a great way to practise your **vocabulary** skills.

Take Five

Look at the words on the left and circle all five synonyms for each word in the boxes on the right. Unscramble the bold letters to reveal a word, and write the word on the line below.

INFORM

jus**ti**fy   report   a**d**vise   edu**c**ate
shout   **n**otify   obse**r**ve   **a**pprise

HORRIBLE

vile   gh**a**stly   reckless   preten**t**ious
inept   **u**npleasant   repul**s**ive   mali**c**ious

The unscrambled word is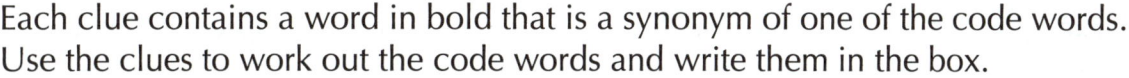

Hint: the word is an antonym of 'deliberate'.

Monkeying Around

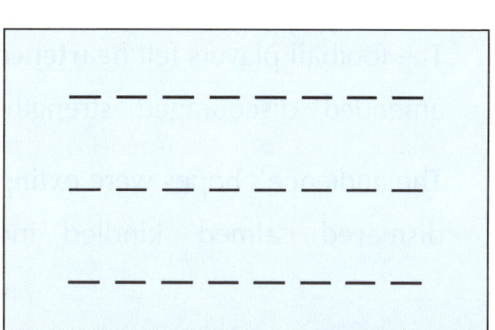

Gerald has forgotten the three code words to his banana safe. Each code word starts with the same letter as his name, and Gerald has some clues to help him remember them.

Each clue contains a word in bold that is a synonym of one of the code words. Use the clues to work out the code words and write them in the box.

1. Chip the chimpanzee will believe anything — he's **naive**.

2. Chip is a wonderful dancer — he's **elegant**.

3. Chip always shares his bananas with me — he's **unselfish**.

Test 3

You have **10 minutes** to do this test. Work as quickly and as accurately as you can.

Underline a word from the first set, followed by a word from the second set, that go together to form a new word.

Example: (<u>water</u> suggest disc) (<u>fall</u> hard ton)   (The word is **waterfall**.)

1. (stage enter glare)   (trance ring prise)
2. (up over fur)   (owe lode roar)
3. (for after too)   (thought night live)
4. (bed bead heed)   (stone rock rag)
5. (plot pollute accept)   (ants age able)
6. (heir handle heel)   (brush loom tear)
7. (skills way inn)   (set put laid)

Underline the word that is the best antonym for the word in bold and makes sense in the sentence.

Example: Peter found the visit **dull**.   <u>exciting</u> dreary upsetting boring

8. The football players felt **heartened** when they saw the scoreboard.
   amended discouraged strengthened disconcerted

9. The audience's hopes were **extinguished** by the politician's speech.
   dismayed calmed kindled indulged

10. Tina was surprised by the **tranquillity** of the sea.
    placidity   turmoil   momentum   consternation

11. The **friendship** between the two brothers was clear to see.
    affection   animosity   moderation   repression

12. The council's efforts could **mitigate** the problem.
    compound   clear   recognise   initiate

13. Harrison thought his job was **odious**.
    fulfilling   worthless   instructive   delightful

Complete the word on the right so that it is a synonym, or nearly a synonym, of the word on the left.

Example: rug   c a r p e t

14. questionable   d _ b i _ _ s
15. district   _ e _ i o _
16. durable   _ _ s t _ _ g
17. demonstrate   _ x h _ _ i t
18. celebration   r _ v e _ _ y
19. bandit   _ _ _ _ l w

> Look at the word on the left. Underline the category that it belongs to.
>
> **Example**: scarlet   <u>red</u>   yellow   blue   green

20. rib   muscle   bone   tissue   limb

21. swarm   product   feeling   animal   group

22. orchid   flower   bag   colour   fruit

23. cardigan   accessory   garment   jewellery   footwear

24. artichoke   bean   vegetable   protein   dessert

25. sister   acquaintance   colleague   sibling   comrade

END OF TEST

/ 25

Test 4

You have **10 minutes** to do this test. Work as quickly and as accurately as you can.

> Three of the words in each list are linked. Mark the word that is not related to these three.
>
> **Example**:   teacher   doctor   <u>hospital</u>   firefighter

1. road   trail   journey   pathway

2. emperor   minister   king   sultan

3. braided   knotted   welded   plaited

4. tower   overshadow   eclipse   outshine

5. station   travel   stop   destination

6. friendly   welcoming   warm   civil

> Underline the correct homophone to complete the sentence.
>
> **Example**:   Archie tied a _____ in the ship's rigging.   not   <u>knot</u>

7. The horse shook its shaggy _____.   mane   main

8. Bryn opened a _____ in his desk.   draw   drawer

9. The country was in _____ for the king.   morning   mourning

10. The film made millions in _____.   prophet   profit

11. Emeka was stuck in _____ traffic.   stationary   stationery

12. First, write a _____ of your essay.   draft   draught

13. She _____ all her courage.   mustard   mustered

Underline the word that is the best synonym for the word in bold and makes sense in the sentence.

Example: The river was **broad**.   flowing   muddy   <u>wide</u>   fast

---

14. The lawyer **questioned** the judge's decision.
    analysed   challenged   acknowledged   enquired

15. The view from the mountain's summit was **astounding**.
    astonishing   distressing   beautiful   alarming

16. As he stood up to sing, the lyrics to his solo **eluded** him.
    avoided   escaped   struck   bewildered

17. Sara gasped when she opened the box to find a **delicate**, jewelled necklace.
    sparkling   vintage   sickly   fragile

18. Max's **dream** was to be on the school council.
    ambition   demand   motive   diligence

19. Smruti thought it was **catastrophic** that her flight had been cancelled.
    inconsolable   predictable   disastrous   frustrating

Look at the definition on the left. Underline the word on the right that best matches the definition.

Example: to jog slowly   scurry   lunge   sprint   <u>trot</u>

20. to make clear   lecture   emblazon   <u>clarify</u>   vocalise

21. friendly in nature   discerning   vivacious   <u>amicable</u>   accustomed

22. a lack of energy   <u>lethargy</u>   monotone   avail   amenity

23. to take apart   disfavour   constitute   disorder   <u>disassemble</u>

24. to end a disturbance   buttress   <u>quell</u>   culminate   dignify

25. underhand and sneaky   forthright   <u>devious</u>   steadfast   irresolute

END OF TEST

/ 25

Puzzles 2

Time for a break! This puzzle is a great way to practise your **word-making** skills.

Alphabet Soup

Indira wants to split the pot of alphabet soup below into four different bowls. Each bowl must have four words in it. The labels above the bowls tell you how many letters the words in each bowl should have.

The letters should only be used once per word.

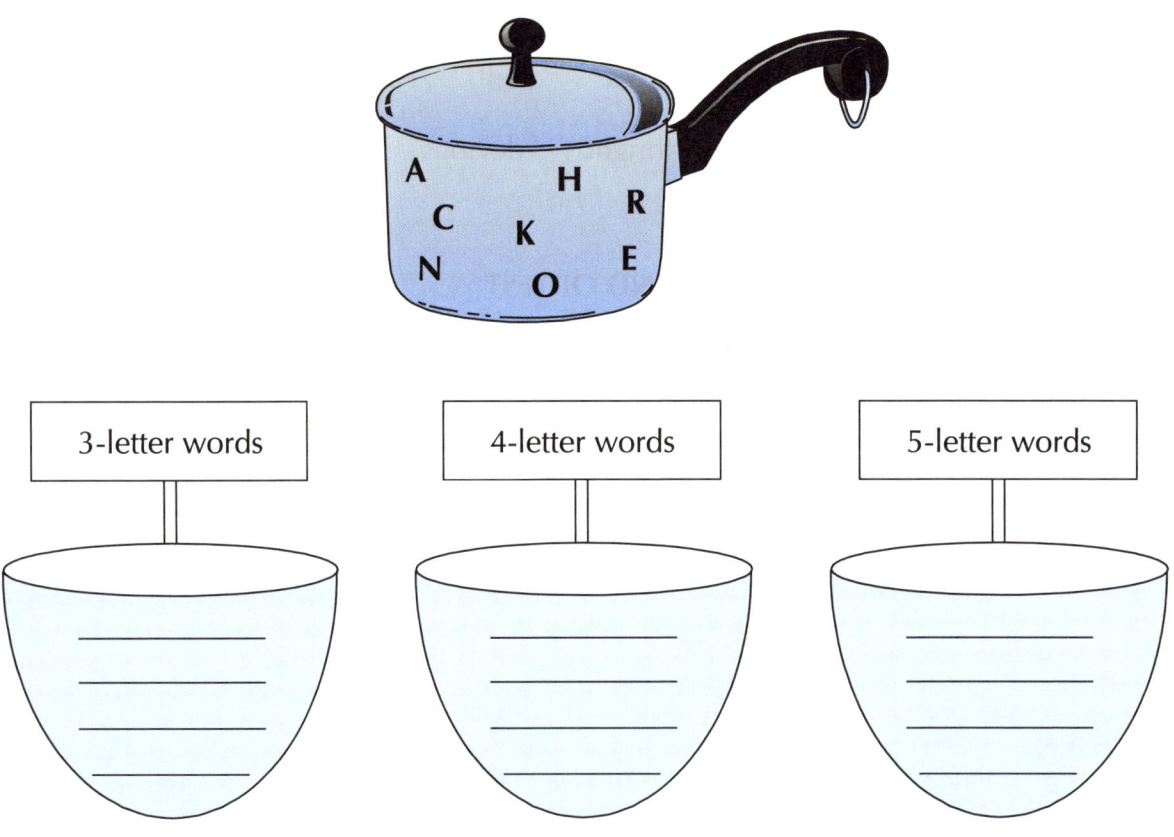

3-letter words

4-letter words

5-letter words

There's also a six-letter word in the soup that means 'fasten securely'. Can you find it? Write it on the line below.

Test 5

10 minutes

You have **10 minutes** to do this test. Work as quickly and as accurately as you can.

> Underline a word from the first set, followed by a word from the second set, that go together to form a new word.
>
> **Example**: (<u>water</u> suggest disc) (<u>fall</u> hard ton)   (The word is **waterfall**.)

1. (tap miss time)   (take scale measure)

2. (coin feed paid)   (charge rest back)

3. (clip photo snap)   (chute shot hit)

4. (spell magic draw)   (catch bound hold)

5. (sin bane mini)   (stair on up)

6. (sign war board)   (rant all mine)

> Look at the word on the left. Underline the category that it belongs to.
>
> **Example**: scarlet   <u>red</u>   yellow   blue   green

7. cello   instrument   machine   vehicle   singer

8. limerick   novel   poem   film   play

9. microwave   furniture   structure   decoration   appliance

10. Africa   country   continent   state   republic

11. lobster   reptile   amphibian   shellfish   oyster

12. chiffon   fabric   cat   cloud   metal

Complete the word on the right so that it is an antonym, or nearly an antonym, of the word on the left.

Example: smooth   r_oug_h

13. adore   _____test

14. mandatory   volu_____

15. mystify   enl_____en

16. sincerely   dec_____ully

17. commencement   con_____sion

18. compassionate   unfe_____g

19. extraordinary   a_____ge

Underline the word that is the best synonym for the word in bold and makes sense in the sentence.

Example: The river was **broad**.   flowing   muddy   <u>wide</u>   fast

20. Dev's character plays an **integral** part in the film's plot.
    interesting   unnecessary   compulsory   essential

21. Haley was tired of listening to Amanda's **nonsense**.
    dross   drivel   detritus   chatter

22. The new sports centre was quite a **substantial** building.
    imposing   unattractive   sizeable   controversial

Test 5

23. The knight **begged** the lord to show mercy.
    implored   reasoned   petitioned   charged

24. It was **evident** that the team hadn't put in their best performance.
    proof   suggested   apparent   glaring

25. They stumbled across a **dilapidated** cottage in the forest.
    charming   ramshackle   abandoned   trembling

END OF TEST

/ 25

Test 6

You have **10 minutes** to do this test. Work as quickly and as accurately as you can.

Underline a word from the first set, followed by a word from the second set, that go together to form a new word.

Example: (<u>water</u> suggest disc) (<u>fall</u> hard ton) (The word is **waterfall**.)

1. (up sun red)   (rite bath dial)
2. (end die rein)   (court vest close)
3. (care full just)   (able loss ice)
4. (miss fore tar)   (sale get make)
5. (weak water of)   (tight spring end)

Look at the definition on the left. Underline the word on the right that best matches the definition.

Example: to jog slowly   scurry   lunge   sprint   <u>trot</u>

6. mild in nature   benign   surly   compelling   honourable
7. a period of calm   posture   fete   serendipity   lull
8. to go around   intersect migrate   proceed   circumnavigate
9. firmness of character   melodrama grit   pursuit   turmoil
10. a story with a moral   prayer   legend   figment   parable

Test 6

Select the most appropriate word from the table to complete each pair of antonyms below. Write the word on the corresponding line.

| furious | order | contrast | pollute | rationally |
| radically | supple | convince | faultless | recede |

11. illogically   _____
12. defective   _____
13. advance   _____
14. mayhem   _____
15. cleanse   _____

16. rigid   _____
17. moderately   _____
18. dissuade   _____
19. placid   _____
20. resemblance   _____

Complete the word on the right so that it is a synonym, or nearly a synonym, of the word on the left.

Example: rug   __car__pet

21. delinquent   of_____er
22. verdict   _____ision
23. recollection   m_____y
24. affiliated   rel_____ed
25. obedient   d_____ile

END OF TEST

/ 25

Test 7

You have **10 minutes** to do this test. Work as quickly and as accurately as you can.

> Find the word that is a synonym, or nearly a synonym, of the word on the left.
>
> **Example**: **wide**   flat   straight   <u>broad</u>   long

1. **occurrence**   disaster   event   mistake   recollect
2. **sleek**   slimy   radiant   silky   grainy
3. **diligently**   maniacally   conscientiously   smoothly   mildly
4. **flawed**   exacting   unsound   feigned   tedious
5. **ascend**   deserve   agree   explore   rise
6. **scurry**   sneak   scamper   dawdle   step

> Three of the words in each list are linked. Mark the word that is not related to these three.
>
> **Example**: teacher   doctor   <u>hospital</u>   firefighter

7. acorn   willow   chestnut   birch
8. decay   split   smash   crack
9. freeze   melt   vapour   evaporate
10. platform   stage   scaffold   tunnel
11. bizarre   standard   peculiar   atypical
12. elated   joyful   composed   buoyant

Underline the word that is the best antonym for the word in bold and makes sense in the sentence.

Example: Peter found the visit **dull**.   <u>exciting</u>   dreary   upsetting   boring

13. Mabel thought her daughter's idea was **viable**.
    potential   impractical   extolled   enigmatic

14. The wooden floor had a certain **sheen**.
    dullness   vulgarity   smoothness   density

15. Cassie was **objective** when she judged the competition.
    biased   detached   inaccurate   ambivalent

16. There was no **accord** in the group about how to proceed.
    conformity   conflict   indiscretion   perception

17. Daisy **conceded** that it was her fault.
    speculated   confessed   denied   resisted

18. Khalid's writing was good, but his poetry was **mediocre**.
    inferior   exceptional   intermediate   principal

Mark the word outside the brackets that has a similar meaning to the words in both sets of brackets.

Example: (find discover) (stain blemish)   freckle   smudge   <u>spot</u>   see

19. (topic theme)   (vulnerable liable)   subject   concept   content   matter

20. (drill pierce)   (nuisance bother)   gouge   drag   bore   pain

21. (spell duration)   (word expression)   phase session course term

22. (stomp trample)   (imprint impress)   stamp insignia crush etch

23. (climb mount)   (spectrum ranking)   scramble rating scale scope

24. (offset counteract)   (symmetry harmony)   balance redress cancel rate

25. (voyage crossing)   (corridor walkway)   aisle passage alleyway cruise

END OF TEST

/ 25

Puzzles 3

Time for a break! These puzzles are a great way to practise your **spelling** skills.

Write It Right

The four sentences below are each missing two homophones. Write the missing homophones in the gaps below, but make sure you spell them correctly.

1. The model [pl_____] has no design on it — it is very [pl_____].

2. Mum says [p_____e] makes perfect, so I [p_____e] the viola every day.

3. The farmer had to [s_____] up the hole in his sock before going outside to [s_____] seeds in the field.

Rory's Story

Some words are missing from Rory's story. Each missing word has one letter different from the previous missing word. Fill in the gaps with the correct words. The first missing word is one letter different from the word 'tale'.

Euan's face turned _____ when the _____ of laundry on the floor started to move towards him. He jumped a _____ in the air, knocking a glass of _____ over. A _____ blouse lunged out of the laundry and grabbed his leg. He managed to wriggle away from the soft fabric, but it attacked again and started to laugh. Euan began to _____ when he realised the monster was just his sister!

Test 8

You have **10 minutes** to do this test. Work as quickly and as accurately as you can.

Choose the correct three-letter word to complete the word in capital letters, so that it finishes the sentence in a sensible way.

Example: It can be **CHY** outside when it snows.

    APP   ILL   EEK   ERR

1. There was a red **BCH** on his skin where the bug had bitten him.

   RUN   RAN   LOT   LEA

2. The biscuits were **SHD** like stars.

   OWE   ARE   APE   ORE

3. Kara ran her hand through the **BES** of grass.

   RUT   LAD   ASH   RIB

4. The plan was **FED**, but it was the best they had.

   LAW   AIL   AIR   LOW

5. The fierce wind was **BING** through the trees.

   LOW   AND   OAT   DIN

6. The outline of the house was clearly **DEED** against the sky.

   LUG   BIT   BAT   FIN

Look at the word on the left. Underline the category that it belongs to.

Example: scarlet   <u>red</u>   yellow   blue   green

7. coffee   liquor   grain   beverage   juice
8. west   direction   destination   compass   vicinity
9. spoon   saucer   cutlery   crockery   knife
10. tournament   test   race   sport   competition
11. petrol   energy   rocket   fuel   fire
12. adjective   speech   sentence   word   punctuation
13. staple   stencil   stationery   utensil   template

Complete the word on the right so that it is an antonym, or nearly an antonym, of the word on the left.

Example: smooth   r o u g h

14. insignificant   m _ m _ _ _ o u s
15. punish   p _ r _ _ n
16. flippant   s _ _ i _ _ s
17. illuminate   _ _ r k _ n
18. acceptance   d _ _ i a _
19. humility   a _ r o _ _ n c e

25   Test 8

Find the word that is a synonym, or nearly a synonym, of the word on the left.

Example: **wide** flat straight <u>broad</u> long

20. **contradict**   contribute   oppose   consent   omit

21. **contempt**   sanction   acclaim   disdain   fury

22. **incessant**   enraged   continual   unreasonable   abiding

23. **briskly**   vigorously   violently   hectically   determinedly

24. **variety**   assortment   system   arrangement   separation

25. **virtue**   veracity   merit   feat   reality

END OF TEST

Test 9

You have **10 minutes** to do this test. Work as quickly and as accurately as you can.

> Underline the correct homophone to complete the sentence.
>
> **Example**:   Archie tied a _____ in the ship's rigging.   not   <u>knot</u>

1. The boxer stepped into the _____.   wring   ring
2. You can _____ food to keep it fresh.   frees   freeze   frieze
3. The car was getting _____ away.   father   farther
4. I had apple crumble for _____.   dessert   desert
5. Tariq _____ his team to victory.   led   lead
6. The aeroplane began its _____.   dissent   descent

> Look at the definition on the left. Underline the word on the right that best matches the definition.
>
> **Example**:   to jog slowly   scurry   lunge   sprint   <u>trot</u>

7. to send out   transmute   retain   instigate   transmit
8. a liking for   affinity   endorsement   union   reference
9. to grow strongly   prevail   heighten   conquer   thrive
10. related to death   malicious   gaunt   macabre   barren
11. to give up   forfeit   obliterate   transgress   subdue
12. to make known   disclose   deny   disown   enunciate

Complete the word on the right so that it is a synonym, or nearly a synonym, of the word on the left.

Example: rug   __car__ pet

13. isolation   _____lusion

14. strict   s_____re

15. collaboration   tea_____k

16. define   _____cify

17. rustic   ru_____l

18. remark   co_____t

19. pinpoint   _____tify

Underline the word that is the best antonym for the word in bold and makes sense in the sentence.

Example: Peter found the visit **dull**.   <u>exciting</u>   dreary   upsetting   boring

20. The writer was **condemned** by critics for his latest book.
    lauded   attained   cultivated   criticised

21. The machine's operating instructions were **comprehensible**.
    inappropriate   unintelligible   incomplete   cogent

22. Hannah maintained her **enthusiasm** all day.
    admiration   dereliction   vehemence   apathy

23. The rabbit was **concealed** next to the hedge.
    precise   palpable   indistinct   exposed

24. When he did his homework, Adrian was **immune** to distractions.
    culpable   susceptible   unsullied   attested

25. Jessica thought that her neighbour was quite **sullen**.
    malevolent   hapless   simpering   cheery

END OF TEST

/ 25

Test 10

You have **10 minutes** to do this test. Work as quickly and as accurately as you can.

Mark the word outside the brackets that has a similar meaning to the words in both sets of brackets.

Example: (find discover) (stain blemish)   freckle   smudge   <u>spot</u>   see

1. (harvest gather)   (choice selection)   pluck   elect   pick   prize
2. (clutter jumble)   (brood offspring)   detritus   strew   issue   litter
3. (basket crate)   (frustrate curb)   punnet   thwart   hamper   block
4. (crouch stoop)   (inkling feeling)   hunch   suspicion   protrusion   jut
5. (area discipline)   (meadow pasture)   sphere   range   field   partition

Underline a word from the first set, followed by a word from the second set, that go together to form a new word.

Example: (<u>water</u> suggest disc) (<u>fall</u> hard ton)   (The word is **waterfall**.)

6. (mind brain care)   (rest warn wash)
7. (turned off head)   (tail light over)
8. (view see stop)   (point line find)
9. (disc for in)   (time ever close)
10. (meaning change brake)   (full able ship)

Select the most appropriate word from the table to complete each pair of synonyms below. Write the word on the corresponding line.

daring	skilful	paradise	significance	berate
bargain	veneer	conspire	assess	uninspiring

11. collude _____

12. lacklustre _____

13. negotiate _____

14. adept _____

15. magnitude _____

16. chide _____

17. intrepid _____

18. appraise _____

19. utopia _____

20. appearance _____

Complete the word on the right so that it is an antonym, or nearly an antonym, of the word on the left.

Example: smooth   r_oug_h

21. rebel   co_____ly

22. favour   dis_____val

23. confine   _____ease

24. wasteful   ec_____ical

25. fidelity   disl_____y

END OF TEST

/ 25

Puzzles 4

Time for a break! These puzzles are a great way to practise your **word-making** skills.

Puzzling Prefixes

Each of the prefixes on the left can be added to one of the incomplete words in the middle to make a new word that matches the definition on the right. Fill in the missing letters in the words then draw an arrow from each prefix to the correct word and definition.

dis	☐ n n ☐ c t	→	to join two pieces together again
re	s ☐ c ☐ r ☐	→	unsafe or unstable
un	m ☐ ☐ k ☐ d	→	without distinguishing marks
in	☐ a t ☐ ☐ f y	→	to fail to please

Twin-onyms

Maisy and Daisy are identical twins with very similar personalities. Unjumble the words that they've used to describe themselves, then draw a line to match the synonyms.

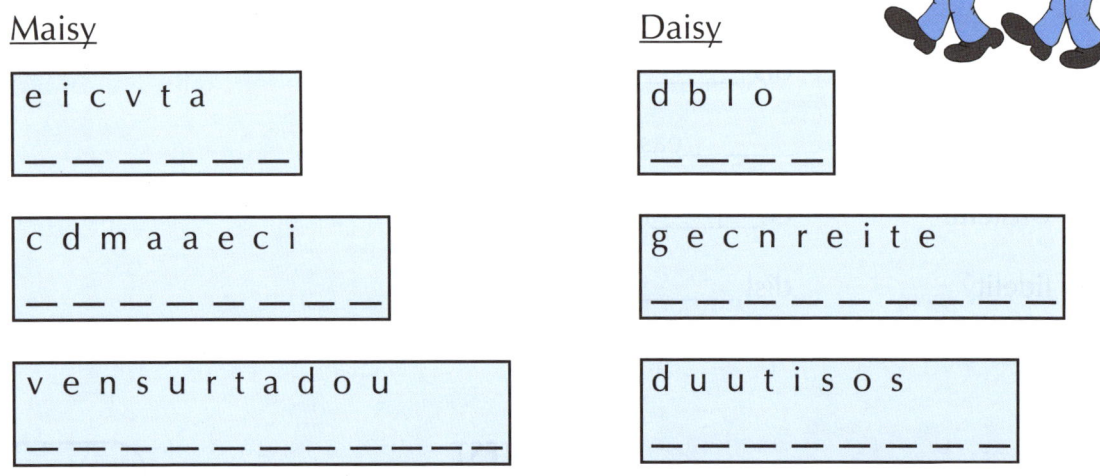

Maisy

e i c v t a
_ _ _ _ _ _

c d m a a e c i
_ _ _ _ _ _ _ _

v e n s u r t a d o u
_ _ _ _ _ _ _ _ _ _ _

Daisy

d b l o
_ _ _ _

g e c n r e i t e
_ _ _ _ _ _ _ _ _

d u u t i s o s
_ _ _ _ _ _ _ _

Test 11

You have **10 minutes** to do this test. Work as quickly and as accurately as you can.

Underline the correct homophone to complete the sentence.

Example: Archie tied a _____ in the ship's rigging.   not   knot

1. Deepa hoped she had _____ taller.   grown   groan
2. Erik was the only _____ in the hotel.   guest   guessed
3. Mel played a _____ on the guitar.   cored   chord   cord
4. I wore a glittery dress to the _____.   bawl   ball
5. A fire was burning in the _____.   great   grate
6. Niamh fitted a new carpet on the _____.   stairs   stares

Mark the word outside the brackets that has a similar meaning to the words in both sets of brackets.

Example: (find discover) (stain blemish)   freckle   smudge   spot   see

7. (structure shape)   (construct create)   form   pattern   design   blueprint
8. (brawl clash)   (wear unravel)   fray   rip   rampage   tussle
9. (tide flow)   (modern contemporary)   stream   flood   topical   current
10. (shear crop)   (cutting excerpt)   dock   trim   clip   quote
11. (stake part)   (apportion split)   distribute   share   bit   dividend
12. (array position)   (schedule organise)   file   arrange   locate   order

Find the word that is an antonym, or nearly an antonym, of the word on the left.

Example: **first**   later   <u>last</u>   next   beginning

13. **reward**   correlate   penalise   reproach   commend
14. **eternal**   instantaneous   infinite   fleeting   preceding
15. **resist**   prolong   yield   toil   compromise
16. **deserted**   inhabited   fruitful   parched   accessible
17. **ancestor**   forebear   descendant   sibling   precursor
18. **raucous**   turbulent   resigned   sluggish   hushed
19. **seldom**   sporadically   frequently   permanently   variously

Underline the word that is the best synonym for the word in bold and makes sense in the sentence.

Example: The river was **broad**.   flowing   muddy   <u>wide</u>   fast

20. The group of outlaws **plotted** to commit shocking crimes.
    connived   attempted   insinuated   resolved

21. Cara was **determined** that she should deliver the speech.
    decisive   stalwart   adamant   declined

22. The restaurant was **noted** for its delicious desserts.
    acclaimed   visited   highlighted   advertised

23. Kyle felt **privileged** to be in the school play.
    honoured   impelled   embarrassed   prospered

24. Detective Chun began his **interrogation**.
    inspection   inquisition   appraisal   determination

25. Taking photographs is **forbidden** inside the museum.
    encouraged   denigrated   affirmative   prohibited

END OF TEST

/ 25

Test 12

You have **10 minutes** to do this test. Work as quickly and as accurately as you can.

> Choose the correct three-letter word to complete the word in capital letters, so that it finishes the sentence in a sensible way.
>
> **Example**: It can be **CHY** outside when it snows.
>
> APP   ILL ▪   EEK   ERR

1. Eleanor's house was in the **HIEST** part of the village.

   OAR   APP   ILL   AIR

2. Freya's pet tortoise was **DLY** loved by her family.

   AFT   EAR   IRE   OUR

3. The squirrel **DED** out from behind the tree.

   MAN   ART   OWN   FEN

4. Emily rented two **CAS** for her family to stay in.

   PER   BIN   USE   SHE

5. The dress shop was sold out of **SES**.

   ASH   CON   HAM   WED

Select the most appropriate word from the table to complete each pair of antonyms below. Write the word on the corresponding line.

artificial	calm	accepted	alienate	excess
assertive	prudence	obstruct	ridiculous	undetected

6. folly   _____
7. declined   _____
8. genuine   _____
9. sensible   _____
10. perceived   _____

11. unblock   _____
12. include   _____
13. submissive   _____
14. dearth   _____
15. agitation   _____

Complete the word on the right so that it is a synonym, or nearly a synonym, of the word on the left.

Example: rug   __car__pet

16. nominate   rec_____nd
17. literate   ed_____ted
18. accompany   esc_____
19. courier   me_____ger
20. power   aut_____ty

Test 12

> Look at the word on the left. Underline the category that it belongs to.
>
> **Example**: scarlet   <u>red</u>   yellow   blue   green

21. anorak   <u>coat</u>   shoe   shirt   hat

22. Venus   asteroid   <u>goddess</u>   artist   moon

23. Euro   <u>currency</u>   bank   government   country

24. encore   conductor   tool   journey   <u>performance</u>

25. sculpture   <u>carving</u>   cliff   frame   marble

END OF TEST

/ 25

Test 13

10 minutes

You have **10 minutes** to do this test. Work as quickly and as accurately as you can.

> Complete the word on the right so that it is an antonym, or nearly an antonym, of the word on the left.
>
> **Example:** smooth   r o u g h

1. formal   _ a s _ _ l
2. recklessness   _ a u _ i _ n
3. maturity   _ _ u t h
4. advisable   u _ w _ _ e
5. calmness   _ _ m m _ t i _ n
6. airy   _ t _ f f _
7. construct   w _ e _ _

> Three of the words in each list are linked. Mark the word that is not related to these three.
>
> **Example:** teacher   doctor   <u>hospital</u>   firefighter

8. frank   basic   plain   direct
9. sentence   clause   spelling   phrase
10. darn   needle   embroider   stitch

11. entrust   exonerate   vindicate   acquit

12. credibly   plausibly   believably   excusably

13. duke   countess   baroness   dame

> Underline the word that is the best synonym for the word in bold and makes sense in the sentence.
>
> **Example**:   The river was **broad**.   flowing   muddy   <u>wide</u>   fast

14. Yesterday, I listened to a **fascinating** interview on the radio.
    conceited   intriguing   thrilling   alluring

15. Tourists flock to visit the **magnificent** castle.
    bewitching   expansive   majestic   sonorous

16. The athletes have a **gruelling** training schedule.
    detailed   dynamic   laborious   comprehensive

17. Robin was **chastised** for his selfish behaviour.
    scolded   endorsed   advised   expounded

18. Mrs Sharma's class had behaved **despicably** all day.
    impeccably   abominably   strangely   obstinately

19. The garden **withered** while the gardener was on holiday.
    languished   flourished   renewed   ripened

> Look at the definition on the left. Underline the word on the right that best matches the definition.
>
> **Example**: to jog slowly   scurry   lunge   sprint   <u>trot</u>

20. to spread through   permeate   siphon   surge   emerge

21. leaving no doubt   candid   disputable   unequivocal   sceptical

22. using strategy   considerate   tactical   tenacious   valiant

23. local language   dialect   abbreviation   vocabulary   maxim

24. to move stealthily   swoop   totter   clamber   creep

25. great height   optimum   stature   altitude   aerial

END OF TEST

/ 25

Puzzles 5

Time for a break! These puzzles are a great way to practise your **vocabulary** skills.

Befuddled Basketballs

A clumsy pupil has knocked all of the school's basketballs off their racks. Each ball must go next to a ball that has a word that means the same, or nearly the same, as the word on the ball before it. Use the balls on the right to fill in the two sets of missing words below. Some of the balls have been put back for you.

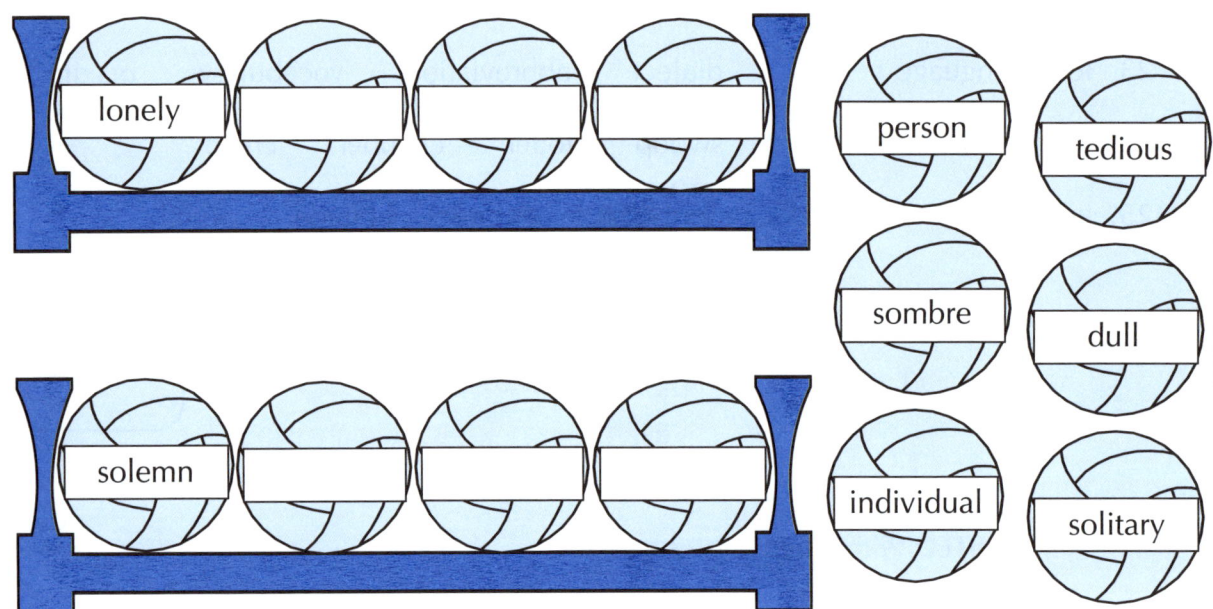

lonely _____ _____ _____

solemn _____ _____ _____

Bird is the Word

Remove between two and eight letters from each of the following words to leave a word that is related to the topic of birds.

e̶g̶regious   fully   sneakiest

         willing   promisingly

egg   _____   _____

_____   _____

Test 14

You have **10 minutes** to do this test. Work as quickly and as accurately as you can.

Choose the correct three-letter word to complete the word in capital letters, so that it finishes the sentence in a sensible way.

Example: It can be **CHY** outside when it snows.

    APP   ILL   EEK   ERR

1. Hector **DECS** the liquid into separate glasses.

   ODE   LAW   ANT   AMP

2. Fill in your occupation, age and **GER** on the form.

   ART   END   AND   LOW

3. The fruit salad was ruined by the **UNE** mango.

   DON   MAD   RIP   ROB

4. Helena **STED** with laughter at the joke.

   MAR   NOR   TUN   WAR

5. Lara **RES** the alarm each time it goes off.

   OUT   SIT   PAY   SET

6. Aled sprinkled the **GED** carrots on top of the salad.

   RIM   RAT   LID   ARE

> Find the word that is an antonym, or nearly an antonym, of the word on the left.
>
> **Example**: **first**　later　<u>last</u>　next　beginning

7. **certainty**　　inaccuracy　possibility　authenticity　oversight

8. **miserly**　　charitable　lenient　churlish　pervasive

9. **incite**　　deter　excite　presume　harass

10. **elegant**　　insensitive　dignified　crude　creative

11. **despondency**　aversion　hopefulness　sensitivity　wonderment

12. **deny**　　authorise　intend　rebuff　involve

> Underline a word from the first set, followed by a word from the second set, that go together to form a new word.
>
> **Example**: (<u>water</u>　suggest　disc)　(<u>fall</u>　hard　ton)　(The word is **waterfall**.)

13. (upper　over　inner)　　(tube　flow　site)

14. (no　street　sum)　　(ware　bodied　thing)

15. (brake　set　make)　　(back　through　down)

16. (miss　see　hear)　　(floor　tier　rank)

17. (for　get　put)　　(over　rid　ate)

18. (dead　fee　full)　　(on　beet　line)

Complete the word on the right so that it is a synonym, or nearly a synonym, of the word on the left.

Example: rug c a r p e t

19. task — a _ s i _ n m _ n _
20. insecure — u _ s _ _ b l _
21. covet — c _ _ v _
22. idealist — d r _ _ m _ _
23. humiliate — m _ r _ i _ y
24. condescending — p _ t _ o _ _ s i n g
25. struggle — _ t r _ v _

END OF TEST

/ 25

Test 15

You have **10 minutes** to do this test. Work as quickly and as accurately as you can.

> Find the word that is a synonym, or nearly a synonym, of the word on the left.
>
> **Example**: wide   flat   straight   <u>broad</u>   long

1. **plentiful**   abundant   unbridled   ambitious   untold
2. **pride**   fortune   conceit   competence   superior
3. **conclude**   congratulate   commence   continue   terminate
4. **original**   authentic   traditional   synthetic   emergent
5. **erratically**   wilfully   conventionally   inconsistently   definitely
6. **fussy**   vague   particular   doubtful   selfish

> Three of the words in each list are linked. Mark the word that is not related to these three.
>
> **Example**: teacher   doctor   <u>hospital</u>   firefighter

7. confiscate   pilfer   embezzle   defraud
8. cyan   sapphire   turquoise   ivory
9. rite   ceremony   routine   service
10. painter   artist   sculptor   illustration
11. ancient   hereditary   antique   elderly
12. address   county   state   region

Look at the word on the left. Underline the category that it belongs to.

Example: scarlet   <u>red</u>   yellow   blue   green

13. elation   personality   emotion   attitude   thought
14. aviator   pilot   engine   athlete   clock
15. wrench   mechanic   screw   bolt   tool
16. chalice   cup   gemstone   clothing   transport
17. paprika   seed   nut   spice   cereal
18. lemon   salad   citrus   herb   condiment

Complete the word on the right so that it is a synonym, or nearly a synonym, of the word on the left.

Example: rug c a r p e t

19. energy   v _ t a _ _ t y
20. promote   a _ v _ _ t i s _
21. vast   c o l _ _ _ _ l
22. quest   _ _ s s _ _ n

23. dishevelled ☐ ☐ k ☐ m p ☐

24. impersonate ☐ i ☐ ☐ c

25. fervent d ☐ ☐ o u ☐

END OF TEST

/ 25

Test 16

You have **10 minutes** to do this test. Work as quickly and as accurately as you can.

Look at the definition on the left. Underline the word on the right that best matches the definition.

Example: to jog slowly   scurry   lunge   sprint   <u>trot</u>

1. elaborately decorated   ornate   pretentious   alluring   impeccable
2. an official assessment   satire   summary   opinion   review
3. causing amusement   caustic   droll   strapping   daunting
4. possessing skill   dexterous   methodical   poignant   acrid
5. a great display   rarity   comedy   spectacle   trinket
6. unable to move   inert   idle   potent   decrepit

Underline a word from the first set, followed by a word from the second set, that go together to form a new word.

Example: (<u>water</u> suggest disc) (<u>fall</u> hard ton) (The word is **waterfall**.)

7. (rein   end   back)   (drop   dive   dear)
8. (super   adult   tight)   (tend   rate   natural)
9. (wrong   often   common)   (done   place   where)
10. (main   some   mean)   (few   while   less)
11. (brow   tent   sense)   (ring   sing   sure)
12. (home   feat   sent)   (her   sure   path)

Complete the word on the right so that it is an antonym, or nearly an antonym, of the word on the left.

Example: smooth   r_oug_h

13. clamour   si_____

14. quit   per_____re

15. universal   _____idual

16. observe   ig_____

17. inexperienced   e_____rt

18. defeated   v_____ious

19. achievable   imp_____le

Underline the word that is the best antonym for the word in bold and makes sense in the sentence.

Example: Peter found the visit **dull**.   <u>exciting</u> dreary upsetting boring

20. The reviews for the new play described it as **monotonous**.
    wooden eventful tiresome academic

21. Ava felt there were **boundless** possibilities to be explored.
    sufficient finite immense trivial

22. Louisa **understated** the scale of the project.
    exaggerated devalued overcame enlarged

23. The performance was **lengthened** when the final song was changed.
    amplified   curtailed   voided   refuted

24. The king knew that his lords were on the verge of **rebellion**.
    liberation   submission   endurance   stupor

25. The castle walls had been **fortified** over the years.
    covered   bastioned   weakened   sophisticated

END OF TEST

/ 25

Puzzles 6

Time for a break! These puzzles are a great way to practise your **vocabulary** skills.

Rhyme Time

There are two groups of incomplete words and two groups of definitions below. Fill in the gaps in the words so that each word matches the definition beside it. The three words defined in each group all rhyme.

v _ r i _ _ a _ _ _ _	can be proved
u _ d _ n i _ _ _ e	impossible to dispute
_ e l _ _ b l _	dependable
_ u s t _ f i _ _ _ e	can be defended

Target Practice

Three of the arrows below can be joined with words on the target to create six new compound words. Find one arrow for each coloured ring of the target. The arrow has to fit with both of the words in the ring to be a correct match.

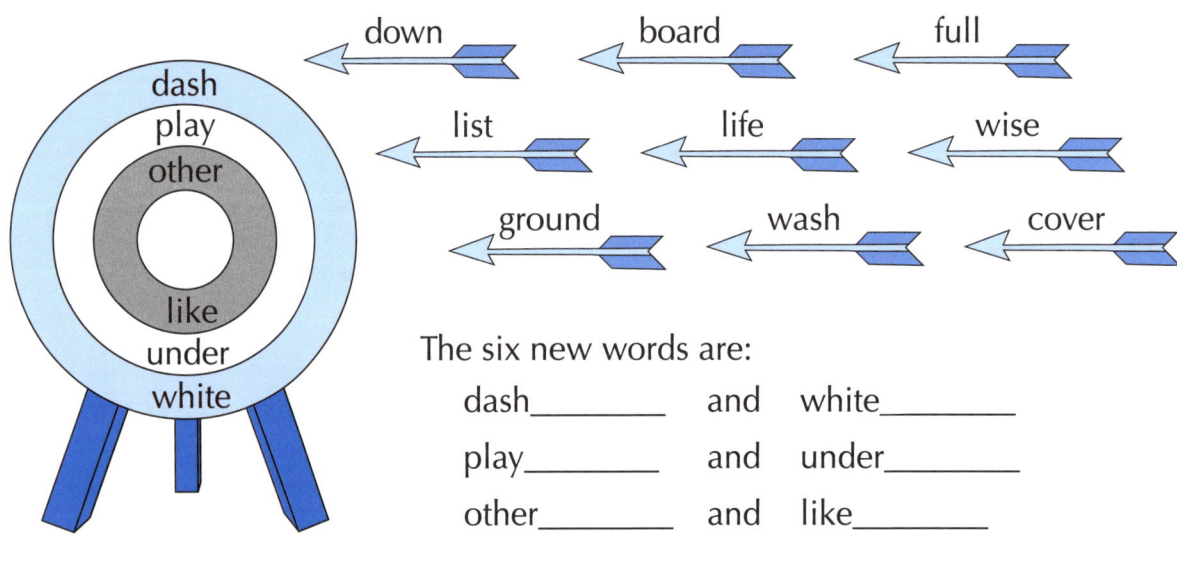

The six new words are:

dash_____ and white_____

play_____ and under_____

other_____ and like_____

Test 17

You have **10 minutes** to do this test. Work as quickly and as accurately as you can.

Underline the correct homophone to complete the sentence.

Example: Archie tied a _____ in the ship's rigging.   not knot

1. This jigsaw is missing a _____!   peace   piece
2. Explain the _____ of using alliteration. affect effect
3. The graze didn't take long to _____.   heel he'll heal
4. Asad cut the _____ cake into slices.   whole   hole
5. She sounded _____ when she spoke.   horse   hoarse

Mark the word outside the brackets that has a similar meaning to the words in both sets of brackets.

Example: (find discover) (stain blemish)   freckle smudge spot see

6. (lesser inferior)   (reduce decrease)   lower drop descend cut
7. (relate connect)   (colleague coworker)   ally join combine associate
8. (trust believe)   (embrace welcome)   accept affirm tolerate infer
9. (symbol rune)   (nature personality)   courage figure character aspect
10. (reject dismiss)   (concession reduction) doubt discount rebate deduct

Select the most appropriate word from the table to complete each pair of antonyms below. Write the word on the corresponding line.

resolutely	significant	subtly	assemble	feeble
hostility	praise	expand	repellent	protruding

11. meaningless _____

12. tentatively _____

13. abbreviate _____

14. criticism _____

15. pleasant _____

16. friendliness _____

17. dismantle _____

18. sunken _____

19. bluntly _____

20. vigorous _____

Complete the word on the right so that it is a synonym, or nearly a synonym, of the word on the left.

Example: rug   __car__ pet

21. flair   st_____

22. cascade   tor_____

23. pause   int_____tion

24. dramatic   _____rical

25. tepid   lu_____rm

END OF TEST

/ 25

Test 18

You have **10 minutes** to do this test. Work as quickly and as accurately as you can.

> Choose the correct three-letter word to complete the word in capital letters, so that it finishes the sentence in a sensible way.
>
> **Example**: It can be **CHY** outside when it snows.
>
>   APP   ILL ■   EEK   ERR

1. The shop has raised its **PRS** on all items since last year.

   LIE   OWE   APE   ICE

2. Boris heard a **TING** noise on the window.

   OUR   APP   EAR   URN

3. I couldn't choose between the different **BRS** of sweets.

   OWN   AID   AND   ACE

4. I heard the **SNS** before I saw the ambulance.

   WOO   PAW   IRE   ARE

5. When her sisters argue, Carys normally **DEFS** the situation.

   END   USE   ACE   EAT

6. Sam **ENS** his brother for being so good at maths.

   SUE   VIE   JOY   ACT

> Three of the words in each list are linked. Mark the word that is not related to these three.
>
> **Example:** teacher   doctor   <u>hospital</u>   firefighter

7. wizardry   witch   warlock   sorcerer

8. blemished   erased   polluted   tarnished

9. hostile   aggressive   threatening   resentful

10. defended   armed   shielded   protected

11. biddable   compliant   passive   bashful

12. emergency   crisis   injury   disaster

> Complete the word on the right so that it is an antonym, or nearly an antonym, of the word on the left.
>
> **Example:** smooth   r<u> oug </u>h

13. disclaim   ac_____edge

14. increase   d_____ction

15. coordinated   cl_____sy

16. courageous   t_____d

17. appease   _____avate

18. dangerous   ha_____ss

19. care   neg_____ce

Test 18 — 56 — © CGP — not to be photocopied

> Find the word that is a synonym, or nearly a synonym, of the word on the left.
>
> **Example**: **wide**   flat   straight   <u>broad</u>   long

20. **grim**   painstaking   dire   exhausting   stale

21. **grateful**   appreciative   impervious   audacious   rewarding

22. **interact**   disregard   communicate   reactivate   concoct

23. **lively**   animated   dispirited   agile   serene

24. **thought**   expectation   faith   creation   notion

25. **stretch**   strain   overdo   dilute   diminish

END OF TEST

/ 25

Test 19

You have **10 minutes** to do this test. Work as quickly and as accurately as you can.

Complete the word on the right so that it is an antonym, or nearly an antonym, of the word on the left.

Example: smooth r o u g h

1. enlarge   d _ m i n _ s _
2. peril   s _ _ _ t y
3. cheer   _ l o _
4. inconspicuous n _ _ i c _ a b l _
5. doubting   _ r _ s _ i n g

Mark the word outside the brackets that has a similar meaning to the words in both sets of brackets.

Example: (find discover) (stain blemish)   freckle smudge <u>spot</u> see

6. (rhythm pulse)   (conquer overcome)   triumph beat metre quash
7. (flower bloom)   (mature evolve)   blossom develop unfold bud
8. (bounce hop)   (obligated constrained) forced propelled hurdle bound
9. (succinct concise) (instruct inform)   prepare advise brief taut
10. (test obstacle)   (confront question)   hazard flout challenge risk

Look at the definition on the left. Underline the word on the right that best matches the definition.

Example: to jog slowly   scurry   lunge   sprint   <u>trot</u>

11. a common saying   advice   slogan   proverb   slander

12. full of energy   spry   airy   rash   stagnant

13. crafty in nature   wily   jaded   worldly   perceptive

14. a smug smile   sneer   smirk   grimace   salute

15. to pull hard   nudge   pressure   wrench   deposit

Select the most appropriate word from the table to complete each pair of synonyms below. Write the word on the corresponding line.

portrayal	control	absorb	eclectic	calling
affirm	dilemma	ludicrous	gift	perceive

16. diverse   _____

17. insist   _____

18. incorporate   _____

19. vocation   _____

20. bequest   _____

21. operate   _____

22. depiction   _____

23. farcical   _____

24. notice   _____

25. quandary   _____

END OF TEST

/ 25

Puzzles 7

Time for a break! This puzzle is a great way to practise your **word-making** skills.

Witch Words

The passage below about Wilma the Witch is missing some words.
Complete the passage using words from the wordsearch. For each word,
circle the word in the wordsearch and fill in the gaps in the passage.

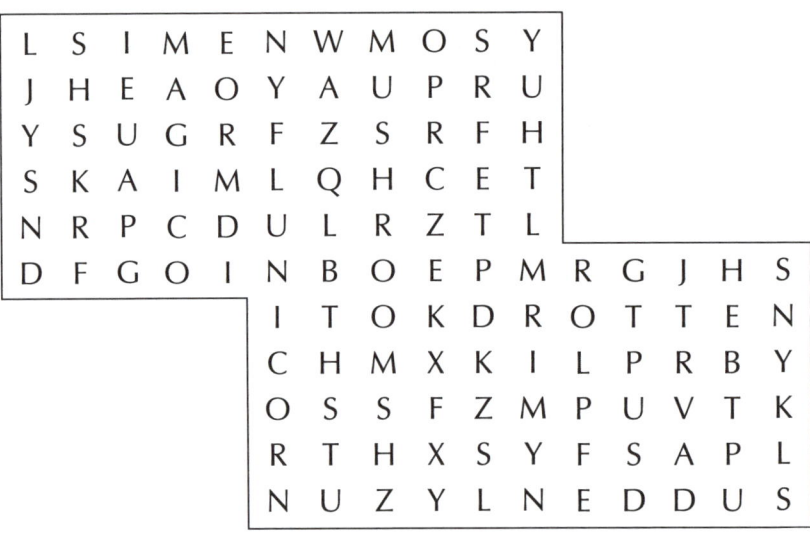

Wilma's house was a __ __ __ __. There were handfuls of __ __ __ __ __ __ __

hair and monster __ __ __ on the carpet and a __ __ __ __ __ __ had spun

an enormous web on the lampshade. Her pet __ __ __ __ __ __ was eating

mouldy __ __ __ __ __ __ __ __ __ and __ __ __ __ __ __ carrots out of the

bin. Wilma knew just what to do. She waved her __ __ __ __ __ wand three

times and everything was __ __ __ __ __ __ __ __ sparkling clean again.

Test 20

You have **10 minutes** to do this test. Work as quickly and as accurately as you can.

Find the word that is an antonym, or nearly an antonym, of the word on the left.

Example: first   later   last   next   beginning

1. **linger**   depart   cease   dominate   repudiate
2. **deplete**   overwhelm   increase   waste   revile
3. **open**   secluded   remote   exposed   extensive
4. **integrity**   dishonesty   injustice   incapacity   decree
5. **central**   peripheral   imminent   relevant   adjacent
6. **precisely**   assuredly   approximately   finally   simply

Underline the correct homophone to complete the sentence.

Example: Archie tied a _____ in the ship's rigging.   not   knot

7. Tim stayed in the hotel's nicest _____.   sweet   suite
8. Pets were _____ from going upstairs.   banned   band
9. Kai pushed the trolley down the _____.   isle   aisle
10. The parcel was _____ to arrive today.   due   dew
11. Nida felt _____ after playing football.   sore   soar   saw
12. Everyone had a different _____ to play.   roll   role

> Complete the word on the right so that it is a synonym, or nearly a synonym, of the word on the left.
>
> **Example:** rug   __car__ pet

13. sentimental   no_____gic

14. competition   ri_____y

15. pathetic   p_____ul

16. explode   _____pt

17. breach   rup_____e

18. talented   g_____ed

19. indicate   sug_____

> Choose the correct three-letter word to complete the word in capital letters, so that it finishes the sentence in a sensible way.
>
> **Example:** It can be **CHY** outside when it snows.
>
>   APP   **ILL**   EEK   ERR

20. In the Second World War, Britain and France were **ALS**.

    WAY   LIE   LOT   TAR

21. The teacher **UNS** a letter from the notice board.

    BAR   ZIP   PIN   TIE

22. The company **INS** extra expenses when it hires more staff.

    CUR   LET   GOT   SET

23. The **RER** sold out the stadium for his concert.

    APP   END   AID   OUT

24. The castle **TRS** over the rest of the city.

    ACT   ONE   AIL   OWE

25. Malia had done her best to be **PREED** for the exam.

    SUM   SAG   FIX   PAR

END OF TEST

/ 25

Test 21

You have **10 minutes** to do this test. Work as quickly and as accurately as you can.

Find the word that is an antonym, or nearly an antonym, of the word on the left.

Example: **first**   later   <u>last</u>   next   beginning

1. **decide**   recommend   waver   fluctuate   surmise
2. **mild**   mellow   supreme   earnest   extreme
3. **uncouth**   natural   refined   crass   pure
4. **variation**   confirmation   semblance   regularity   evasion
5. **renounce**   embrace   commit   entice   concur
6. **smug**   subservient   modest   insolent   confident

Complete the word on the right so that it is a synonym, or nearly a synonym, of the word on the left.

Example: rug   c a r p e t

7. sanctuary   r _ f _ _ e
8. lucrative   _ r _ f i t _ b l _

9. duty   b [ ] [ ] d e [ ]
10. support   a [ ] v [ ] a t e
11. coincidence [ ] l u [ ] e
12. concentrate [ ] [ ] c u [ ]
13. cheerful   j [ ] v [ ] [ ] [ ]

Look at the word on the left. Underline the category that it belongs to.

Example: scarlet   <u>red</u>   yellow   blue   green

14. earl   monarch   manager   aristocrat   empire
15. kidney   organ   illness   vertebra   phase
16. vessel   carriage   hovercraft   boat   car
17. rodent   fowl   biped   insect   mammal
18. Stilton   bread   biscuit   cheese   pasta
19. fraud   punishment   suggestion   rule   offence

Look at the definition on the left. Underline the word on the right that best matches the definition.

Example: to jog slowly   scurry   lunge   sprint   <u>trot</u>

20. to strongly hate   relish   <u>abhor</u>   denounce   prosecute

21. weak in flavour   <u>insipid</u>   temperate   gracious   blasé

22. to make milder   <u>alleviate</u>   agitate   reconcile   purport

23. false appearance   <u>facade</u>   assessment   sensibility   apathy

24. to talk at length   banter   <u>prattle</u>   quibble   bicker

25. to make loose   elucidate   clinch   <u>slacken</u>   submerge

END OF TEST

/ 25

Test 22

You have **10 minutes** to do this test. Work as quickly and as accurately as you can.

> Three of the words in each list are linked. Mark the word that is not related to these three.
>
> **Example**: teacher   doctor   hospital   firefighter

1. resigned   fired   discharged   dismissed
2. organised   efficient   systematic   methodology
3. prophecy   prediction   vision   clairvoyant
4. combat   argument   battle   melee
5. subsequent   following   prior   successive
6. bronze   amethyst   pearl   opal

> Underline a word from the first set, followed by a word from the second set, that go together to form a new word.
>
> **Example**: (water suggest disc) (fall hard ton)   (The word is **waterfall**.)

7. (imp ramp sup)   (part ply load)
8. (fore time worth)   (while loss right)
9. (under other bank)   (account guest estimate)
10. (poll tea prim)   (mate star ate)
11. (over tend thread)   (don bare fare)
12. (thunder storm blow)   (hit struck us)

Look at the word on the left. Underline the category that it belongs to.

Example: scarlet   <u>red</u>   yellow   blue   green

13. herring   fish   music   stone   jewellery
14. hymn   train   monster   song   device
15. boulevard   street   dwelling office   park
16. parasol   forecast shawl   temperature umbrella
17. hamlet   market   settlement urbanisation occupation
18. quill   pen   drawing   pencil   calligraphy
19. slang   behaviour accusation insult language

Underline the word that is the best antonym for the word in bold and makes sense in the sentence.

Example: Peter found the visit **dull**.   <u>exciting</u> dreary upsetting boring

20. Anthony showed **sagacity** in his assessment of the situation.
    stupidity   bitterness   misunderstanding   deflection

21. Owain thought his friend was **inconsiderate** when it came to his needs.
    attentive   unconcerned   dazed   thankless

22. The silence in the village **soothed** Farid.
    repelled   unburdened   disturbed   dishevelled

23. The man was responsible for **initiating** the disturbance.
    halting   instigating   conducting   overthrowing

24. Oni reacted in a **humble** way when she won the award.
    tentative   supercilious   menial   electrifying

25. The outcome of the game demonstrated the team's **strength**.
    asset   frailty   propriety   deference

END OF TEST

/ 25

Puzzles 8

Time for a break! These puzzles are a great way to practise your **vocabulary** skills.

Crack the Code

Kasia is trying to crack the code below. She knows that each letter of the alphabet stands for a different letter. Use the first few letters that she has decoded to help you work out what the code is and write the message below.

A B C D E F G H I J K L M N O P Q R S T U V W X Y Z

W K H   W U H D V X U H   L V
T H E   T R _ _ _ _ _ _ _   _ _

E H Q H D W K   W K H   V K H G
_ _ _ _ _ _ _   _ _ _   _ _ _ _

Mine Mayhem

Mary works in a mine. She has written a report about safety conditions, but some of the words are incomplete. Complete the unfinished words by writing a four-letter word in the blank space on each of the lines below.

Access to the mine is _____**ricted** to mine **em**_____**ees** only.

It is **im**_____**ant** to take proper _____**th** and safety **mea**_____**s**

because the mine can be a dangerous **env**_____**ment**.

These rules apply to **e**_____**one** on site. Please speak

to Mary if you have any questions or **c**_____**rns**.

Test 23

You have **10 minutes** to do this test. Work as quickly and as accurately as you can.

> Underline the correct homophone to complete the sentence.
>
> **Example**: Archie tied a _____ in the ship's rigging. not <u>knot</u>

1. Underline a _____ in this sentence.   clause   claws
2. Carol was the _____ to the estate.   air   heir
3. The phrase had a _____ meaning.   dual   duel
4. The jumper was torn at the _____.   seem   seam
5. She found it hard to _____ the habit.   brake   break
6. Edgar took a walk along the _____.   peer   pier

> Mark the word outside the brackets that has a similar meaning to the words in both sets of brackets.
>
> **Example**: (find discover) (stain blemish)   freckle   smudge   <u>spot</u>   see

7. (indicator meter)   (measure evaluate)   calculate   gauge   dial   signal
8. (candid forthright) (undeviating linear) blunt   expressive   straight   open
9. (extend stretch)   (winch hoist)   device   lift   crane   upend
10. (strain species)   (print lettering)   font   type   category   genre
11. (crack fragment)   (shard sliver)   splinter   particle   burst   blotch
12. (level even)   (quadrangle plaza)   fair   square   court   aligned

Complete the word on the right so that it is an antonym, or nearly an antonym, of the word on the left.

Example: smooth [r][o][u][g][h]

13. inadvertent   [i][n][ ][e][t][ ][t][ ][o][n][ ][l]
14. obey   [d][ ][ ][y]
15. disprove   [ ][o][n][ ][i][ ][m]
16. disarranged   [ ][r][g][a][ ][i][ ][e][d]
17. disagreement [ ][a][r][ ][o][n][ ]
18. sporadic   [ ][ ][g][u][ ][ ][r]

Underline the word that is the best synonym for the word in bold and makes sense in the sentence.

Example: The river was **broad**.   flowing muddy <u>wide</u> fast

19. Bea responded to her brother with **derision**.
    disbelief mockery sorrow annoyance

20. Our Christmas decorations were **ostentatious**.
    unsentimental incredible flamboyant curious

21. The judge had to remain **unbiased** throughout the competition.
    collected impartial concealed separate

22. Jacob **asserted** that his idea was better.
    declared   supposed   mentioned   conceded

23. The main character's family were **penniless**.
    desperate   fruitless   solvent   impoverished

24. Tao was **fascinated** by the nature documentary.
    energised   contravened   enthralled   endeared

25. Lucas gave Nina some **convoluted** directions to the stadium.
    complicated   concise   florid   inaccurate

END OF TEST

/ 25

Test 24

You have **10 minutes** to do this test. Work as quickly and as accurately as you can.

> Find the word that is a synonym, or nearly a synonym, of the word on the left.
>
> **Example**: **wide**   flat   straight   <u>broad</u>   long

1. **base**   foundation   summit   premise   crest
2. **boost**   dwindle   sear   build   jolt
3. **rate**   speed   valuation   span   benefit
4. **possible** tolerable   attainable   passable   reliable
5. **imply**   repress   designate   recall   hint
6. **fine**   serious   subliminal   dainty   rare

> Look at the definition on the left. Underline the word on the right that best matches the definition.
>
> **Example**: to jog slowly   scurry   lunge   sprint   <u>trot</u>

7. very upsetting   harrowing   cunning   perplexing   intense
8. a small irritation   curse   peeve   affliction   torment
9. polite behaviour   convention   etiquette   bigotry   accolade
10. to breathe heavily   splutter   pant   inflate   sigh
11. very courageous   gallant   rapid   prim   vacuous
12. a lack of difficulty   inertia   vigour   facility   flack

Complete the word on the right so that it is an antonym, or nearly an antonym, of the word on the left.

Example: smooth   r_oug_h

13. copious   _____rse

14. vacate   oc_____

15. transparent   op_____ue

16. petty   me_____ful

17. survive   p_____sh

18. energetically   w_____ily

19. presence   abs_____

Choose the correct three-letter word to complete the word in capital letters, so that it finishes the sentence in a sensible way.

Example: It can be CHY outside when it snows.

    APP   ILL   EEK   ERR
    ☐   ■   ☐   ☐

20. The bridesmaid's dress was covered in **FRS**.

    OWN   EVE   ILL   RYE
    ☐   ☐   ☐   ☐

21. Otters have **WED** feet to help them swim.

    EBB   ALL   END   ILL
    ☐   ☐   ☐   ☐

22. The general was **BARG** orders to the troops.

    BIN **DIN** **KIN** **GIN**

23. The **CHS** of the crowd could be heard three streets away.

    EAT **IMP** **AIR** **ANT**

24. Matthew bought some **BETS** in preparation for the picnic.

    ILL **ALL** **RAY** **ASK**

25. Georgia **ADS** working on her art project.

    ORE **MEN** **AGE** **APT**

END OF TEST

/ 25

Test 25

You have **10 minutes** to do this test. Work as quickly and as accurately as you can.

> Mark the word outside the brackets that has a similar meaning to the words in both sets of brackets.
>
> **Example**: (find discover) (stain blemish)   freckle smudge <u>spot</u> see

1. (spy informer)   (freckle mark)   speck agent mole operative
2. (dense tight)   (compress condense)   mini compact squash pressure
3. (sett hole)   (dig tunnel)   burrow lair shelter delve
4. (criminal inmate) (condemn sentence)   accuse convict captive frame
5. (function role)   (employ exercise)   value practice utilise use

> Complete the word on the right so that it is a synonym, or nearly a synonym, of the word on the left.
>
> **Example**:   rug   <u> car </u>pet

6. subdue   su_____ess
7. feud   _____etta
8. uncanny   e_____e
9. laughter   am_____ent
10. tedium   mono_____

Select the most appropriate word from the table to complete each pair of antonyms below. Write the word on the corresponding line.

| suddenly | obscure | humane | restraint | discourtesy |
| arduously | awkward | gaudy | objection | disperse |

11. politeness _____
12. gradually _____
13. approval _____
14. cruel _____
15. gather _____

16. effortlessly _____
17. tasteful _____
18. reveal _____
19. convenient _____
20. indiscipline _____

Look at the word on the left. Underline the category that it belongs to.

Example: scarlet   <u>red</u>   yellow   blue   green

21. ebony   white   black   stone   charcoal
22. riot   agreement   trial   disturbance   setback
23. sergeant   elevation   talent   group   rank
24. molar   tooth   coin   mountain   sword
25. scuffle   dance   wound   fight   scream

END OF TEST

/ 25

Puzzles 9

Time for a break! These puzzles are a great way to practise your **word-making** skills.

Word Builder

Read the definitions below. Work out each word and write it in the blue box. Then add the letters from the white box on the right to make a new, longer word.

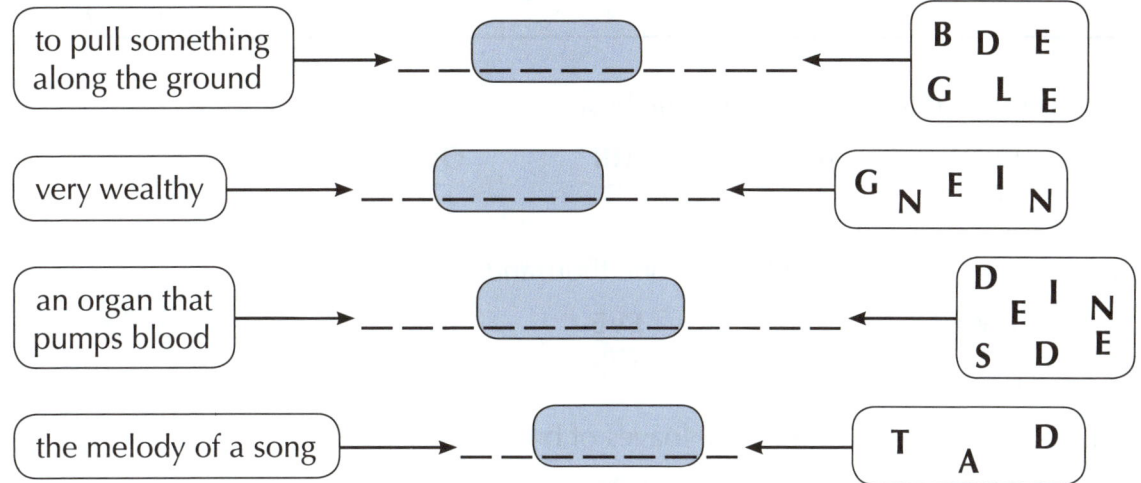

Sign Spellings

The signs below each contain two spelling mistakes. Find the missing letters and write them on the lines on the right, then rearrange the letters to make a word that means 'more snug'.

| **Please be consderate of other pasengers on board.** | _ _ |

| **We sell misellaneous jewellery and precius stones.** | _ _ |

| **Try our signature 'Mediteranean Medly' dish.** | _ _ |

The missing letters spell out the word _ _ _ _ _ _ _

Test 26

You have **10 minutes** to do this test. Work as quickly and as accurately as you can.

Choose the correct three-letter word to complete the word in capital letters, so that it finishes the sentence in a sensible way.

Example: It can be **CHY** outside when it snows.

      APP   **ILL**   EEK   ERR

1. Leon tried to be **FER** to his little brother.

    ODD   ARM   AIR   OLD

2. The average person **BLS** over one thousand times an hour.

    OWE   AGE   EVE   INK

3. Nadia's family **CONE** three loaves of bread every week.

    SUM   DON   LOG   NOT

4. The children recited a **PER** they had learnt.

    EEL   AMP   LAY   RAY

5. Danielle carefully **SED** the envelope.

    ATE   ALE   CON   TAR

6. Derek was **ENED** at the betrayal.

    RAG   COD   ROB   ACT

> Three of the words in each list are linked. Mark the word that is not related to these three.
>
> **Example**: teacher   doctor   hospital   firefighter

7. extortionate   expensive   saleable   pricey

8. sit   kneel   curtsey   bow

9. banquet   consume   meal   feast

10. stench   aroma   scent   fragrance

11. impulsively   hesitantly   spontaneously   instinctively

12. organic   fresh   original   raw

> Find the word that is an antonym, or nearly an antonym, of the word on the left.
>
> **Example**: first   later   last   next   beginning

13. **admire**   scorn   revere   deploy   expire

14. **false**   fictional   literal   faithful   mundane

15. **disappointed** fulfilled   certified   beguiled   disdainful

16. **disgrace**   rebuke   indifference   esteem   curiosity

17. **deluge**   wilt   drought   desiccate   drain

18. **subtle**   visible   imperfect   obvious   mysterious

Complete the word on the right so that it is a synonym, or nearly a synonym, of the word on the left.

Example: rug c a r p e t

19. self-important   p _ m _ _ _ s
20. adapt   a _ j _ _ t
21. poise   c o _ _ _ s u _ e
22. apparel   g _ _ _ e _ t s
23. appreciation   g r _ _ i _ u d _
24. speculate   w _ n _ e _
25. urgent   c _ _ t _ c _ l

END OF TEST

/ 25

Test 27

You have **10 minutes** to do this test. Work as quickly and as accurately as you can.

> Underline the correct homophone to complete the sentence.
>
> **Example**: Archie tied a _____ in the ship's rigging.   not   knot

1. The wine was stored in the _____.   cellar   seller
2. Tristan wanted to _____ the design.   altar   alter
3. The field became a _____ wasteland.   barren   baron
4. Penelope's cat had _____ again.   flees   fleas
5. Maya raced through the obstacle _____.   coarse   course
6. Ash wore a white shirt and blue _____.   genes   jeans

> Underline a word from the first set, followed by a word from the second set, that go together to form a new word.
>
> **Example**: (water suggest disc) (fall hard ton)   (The word is **waterfall**.)

7. (tale high fast)   (light lamp beam)
8. (con fraud mess)   (anger verse pare)
9. (air berth mode)   (score rate cross)
10. (wear where ware)   (out for as)
11. (full awe whole)   (sum sale sell)
12. (sun wind gale)   (ore brake swept)

Complete the word on the right so that it is an antonym, or nearly an antonym, of the word on the left.

Example: smooth [r][o][u][g][h]

13. discourage [ ][o][ ][i][v][a][ ][e]
14. impede [ ][s][s][i][ ][ ]
15. luxury [n][e][ ][e][s][ ][i][t][ ]
16. captivity [f][ ][ ][ ][d][ ][m]
17. interesting [b][ ][ ][ ][d]
18. veteran [n][ ][v][i][ ][ ]
19. reputable [ ][n][f][ ][m][o][u][ ]

Underline the word that is the best synonym for the word in bold and makes sense in the sentence.

Example: The river was **broad**.   flowing muddy <u>wide</u> fast

20. The meeting was full of **powerful** businesspeople.
    renowned   influential   illustrious   reputable

21. Shona found the idea of acting on the stage **exhilarating**.
    menacing   invigorating   inspirational   humorous

22. On completing the trek, the mountaineer suffered from **fatigue**.
    deprivation   exhaustion   drudgery   ailment

Test 27

23. As soon as the bell rang, Noah **promptly** left the classroom.
    mournfully   nonchalantly   swiftly   belatedly

24. Lydia was **devoid** of emotion as she spoke.
    conscious   deficient   ashamed   empty

25. Oli **hesitated** when he saw the queue for the roller coaster.
    persisted   faltered   mediated   refrained

END OF TEST

/ 25

Puzzles 10

Time for a break! These puzzles are a great way to practise your **word-making** skills.

Bubble Trouble

There are 4 eight-letter words hidden in the bubbles below. Read the clues, then draw a line through each column to connect the letters of the word. Each bubble can only be used once. The first connection has been made for you.

1. Something that's entirely correct.
2. A habit or an inclination.
3. Spoken in a displeased tone.
4. Celebrated or expressed delight.

Doughnut Words

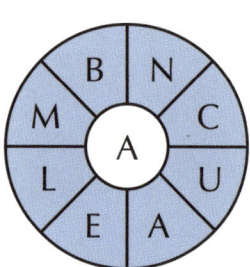

Using only the letters in the doughnut below, find the answers to the clues on the left. Every word must contain the letter 'A', and you can only use each letter once per word.

1. The feeling of being at peace   _ _ _ _ _
2. A type of waterway   _ _ _ _ _ _
3. A gentle walk   _ _ _ _ _ _
4. A book that gives instructions   _ _ _ _ _ _ _ _
5. A type of vehicle   _ _ _ _ _ _ _ _ _ _

Test 28

You have **10 minutes** to do this test. Work as quickly and as accurately as you can.

Look at the word on the left. Underline the category that it belongs to.

Example: scarlet   <u>red</u>   yellow   blue   green

1. quarrel   question   dispute   recommendation   command

2. scholarship   award   decision   service   limitation

3. fondant   brick   weather   icing   light

4. pepper   chemical   seasoning   solution   medicine

Select the most appropriate word from the table to complete each pair of synonyms below. Write the word on the corresponding line.

flaunt	fairly	epiphany	appalling	gathering
stubbornly	obligation	enamoured	coerce	counterfeit

5. horrendous _____   10. commitment _____

6. revelation _____   11. equitably _____

7. parade _____   12. infatuated _____

8. compel _____   13. congregation _____

9. fraudulent _____   14. doggedly _____

Look at the definition on the left. Underline the word on the right that best matches the definition.

Example: to jog slowly   scurry   lunge   sprint   <u>trot</u>

15. very pale   ruddy   lush   <u>ashen</u>   chaste
16. a silly mistake   omission   <u>gaffe</u>   exploitation   spoof
17. to swing wildly   flash   <u>flail</u>   recoil   collide
18. freedom from guilt   adoration   <u>absolution</u>   oblivion   mastery
19. not serious   pertinent   customary   charismatic   <u>frivolous</u>

Underline the word that is the best antonym for the word in bold and makes sense in the sentence.

Example: Peter found the visit **dull**.   <u>exciting</u> dreary upsetting boring

20. Milly's shoes were **outmoded**.
    fabricated   appealing   pungent   <u>fashionable</u>

21. The teacher used **incentives** to help Amir change his behaviour.
    motivations   <u>deterrents</u>   barriers   encouragements

22. Roberta found the metal to be very **inflexible**.
    <u>pliable</u>   fixed   implicit   relentless

23. Rochelle's findings **validated** Becky's theory.
    verified   <u>disproved</u>   altered   confounded

24. Diane had a **concrete** idea about how the picture should look.
    tangible   vague   flimsy   discrete

25. The teacher noticed Lily's **confidence** when speaking to other children.
    arrogance   premonition   diffidence   decorum

END OF TEST

/ 25

Test 29

You have **10 minutes** to do this test. Work as quickly and as accurately as you can.

> Three of the words in each list are linked. Mark the word that is not related to these three.
>
> **Example**: teacher   doctor   <u>hospital</u>   firefighter

1. author   book   poet   playwright
2. immature   infantile   teenager   juvenile
3. takeaway   cafe   bistro   grocer
4. lunge   leap   pounce   gallop
5. limit   deadline   aspiration   restriction
6. embarrass   inhibit   hinder   impede

> Mark the word outside the brackets that has a similar meaning to the words in both sets of brackets.
>
> **Example**: (find discover) (stain blemish)   freckle   smudge   <u>spot</u>   see

7. (contain hold)   (dwelling residence)   house   inhabit   mansion   squat
8. (fluent eloquent)   (express voice)   say   state   articulate   coherent
9. (slump decline)   (ruin demise)   ruination   fall   dip   failure
10. (odd curious)   (comical hysterical)   ironic   unusual   funny   eccentric
11. (parry answer)   (disc token)   relic   dice   counter   utterance
12. (echo evoke)   (remembrance memory)   recall   remind   suspend   ring

Complete the word on the right so that it is an antonym, or nearly an antonym, of the word on the left.

Example: smooth   r_oug_h

13. affluent   de_____ute
14. reject   we_____e
15. vital   opt_____
16. peace   _____cord
17. attach   disc_____ct
18. indefinite   c_____in
19. departure   arr_____

Underline the word that is the best synonym for the word in bold and makes sense in the sentence.

Example: The river was **broad**.   flowing   muddy   <u>wide</u>   fast

20. The players **contemplated** their next move.
    calculated   considered   inspected   pronounced

21. Mr Jenkins saw an **opponent** of his when he was in London.
    contestant   entrant   adversary   accomplice

22. Satnam found the instructions impossible to **comprehend**.
    pursue   fathom   adhere   discern

23. Siân was a **distinguished** member of the ice skating club.
    mythical   conscientious   meticulous   eminent

24. The princess was **banished** from the kingdom.
    exiled   revered   gratified   boycotted

25. Dr Scott devised a brilliant yet **risky** plan.
    precarious   offensive   petrifying   scintillating

END OF TEST

/ 25

Puzzles 11

Time for a break! This puzzle is a great way to practise your **vocabulary** skills.

Whose Dinosaur is Whose?

Read the children's descriptions of their toy dinosaurs in the blue boxes below and unscramble the jumbled words. Look for synonyms in the details beneath each dinosaur to help you work out which dinosaur belongs to which child. Then write the child's name on the line under their dinosaur.

Mindy: My dinosaur is **vosiciu** and **erdegy**.
1ˢᵗ word: v _ _ _ _ _ _ _   2ⁿᵈ word: g _ _ _ _ _ _

Tamal: My dinosaur is **tirreabli** and **lefra**.
1ˢᵗ word: i _ _ _ _ _ _ _ _   2ⁿᵈ word: f _ _ _ _

Felicity: My dinosaur is **surucio** and **ocisblae**.
1ˢᵗ word: c _ _ _ _ _ _   2ⁿᵈ word: s _ _ _ _ _ _ _

RALPH
- bad-tempered
- untamed

_____

REX
- inquisitive
- outgoing

_____

RUBY
- ferocious
- ravenous

_____

Test 30

You have **10 minutes** to do this test. Work as quickly and as accurately as you can.

Choose the correct three-letter word to complete the word in capital letters, so that it finishes the sentence in a sensible way.

Example: It can be **CHY** outside when it snows.

    APP   **ILL**   EEK   ERR

1. Martin always **RES** his bags at the supermarket.

   RUN   USE   ASH   ACT

2. In the past, **QUS** were used for writing.

   ART   ILL   IRK   AIL

3. The fox **PRED** around the garden, looking for food.

   IMP   OWL   APE   ODD

4. The **UNED** question hung in the air between them.

   AIR   WAX   ASK   WAG

5. The snake was **CED** around the branch of a tree.

   OIL   ROW   HIM   LAW

6. Annie **CLED** first prize in the science competition.

   ODD   AMP   ADD   AIM

> Underline the correct homophone to complete the sentence.
>
> **Example**:   Archie tied a _____ in the ship's rigging.   not   <u>knot</u>

7. The dog wagged its _____ happily.   tail   tale
8. Do you know _____ bags these are?   who's   whose
9. Please set out the chairs in _____.   rows   rose
10. There was a _____ flaw in my plan.   miner   minor
11. The cast did a _____ after the show.   bough   bow
12. The _____ house was in disrepair.   manor   manner

> Find the word that is an antonym, or nearly an antonym, of the word on the left.
>
> **Example**:   first   later   <u>last</u>   next   beginning

13. **empower**   invest   undermine   shackle   allege
14. **elevate**   intensify   demote   revolt   extinguish
15. **compliance**   declaration   insistence   disobedience   annulment
16. **coincide**   venerate   differ   rescind   modify
17. **insult**   reproval   insolence   loyalty   compliment
18. **discreet**   hazy   thoughtless   unrestrained   proud

Complete the word on the right so that it is a synonym, or nearly a synonym, of the word on the left.

Example: rug   __car__ pet

19. hallucination   ill_____

20. indefatigable   ti_____ess

21. exasperate   inf_____te

22. competent   qu_____ed

23. loot   _____nder

24. guarantee   p_____dge

25. misrepresent   dis_____t

END OF TEST

/ 25

Test 31

You have **10 minutes** to do this test. Work as quickly and as accurately as you can.

> Find the word that is a synonym, or nearly a synonym, of the word on the left.
>
> **Example**: **wide**   flat   straight   <u>broad</u>   long

1. **quality**   impression   characteristic   category   accessory
2. **late**   punctual   tardy   disinclined   untimely
3. **practical**   futile   challenging   pragmatic   crucial
4. **invent**   orchestrate   fabricate   sabotage   relinquish
5. **abolish**   eradicate   establish   dispatch   reinforce
6. **fantasy**   ordeal   delusion   spectre   trance

> Underline a word from the first set, followed by a word from the second set, that go together to form a new word.
>
> **Example**: (<u>water</u>   suggest   disc)   (<u>fall</u>   hard   ton)   (The word is **waterfall**.)

7. (spy   over   main)   (dive   bear   cooker)
8. (away   on   off)   (jump   spring   time)
9. (far   miles   grave)   (tone   sound   turn)
10. (big   full   main)   (stream   river   wave)
11. (hind   extra   behind)   (trance   sight   vision)
12. (face   look   tails)   (round   pin   about)

Mark the word outside the brackets that has a similar meaning to the words in both sets of brackets.

Example: (find discover) (stain blemish)   freckle smudge <u>spot</u> see

13. (care bother)   (guard protect)   govern tend mind resent

14. (investigate test)   (analysis observation)   experiment proof search check

15. (gravity weight)   (commodity product)   trade worth import freight

16. (shank limb)   (stage segment)   portion foot leg step

17. (only merely)   (merited right)   purely truly equal just

18. (conspiracy plot)   (fascinate absorb)   intrigue appeal delight devise

Complete the word on the right so that it is a synonym, or nearly a synonym, of the word on the left.

Example: rug c a r p e t

19. desist   c _ _ s _

20. terse   b _ u _ _ u e

21. customer   _ _ i e n _

22. exhaustive t h _ _ o u _ _

Test 31   98   © CGP — not to be photocopied

23. scold   [a][ ][m][o][ ][ ][s][h]
24. shameless [ ][r][ ][z][e][ ]
25. hiatus   [i][ ][t][e][ ][v][ ][ ]

END OF TEST

/ 25

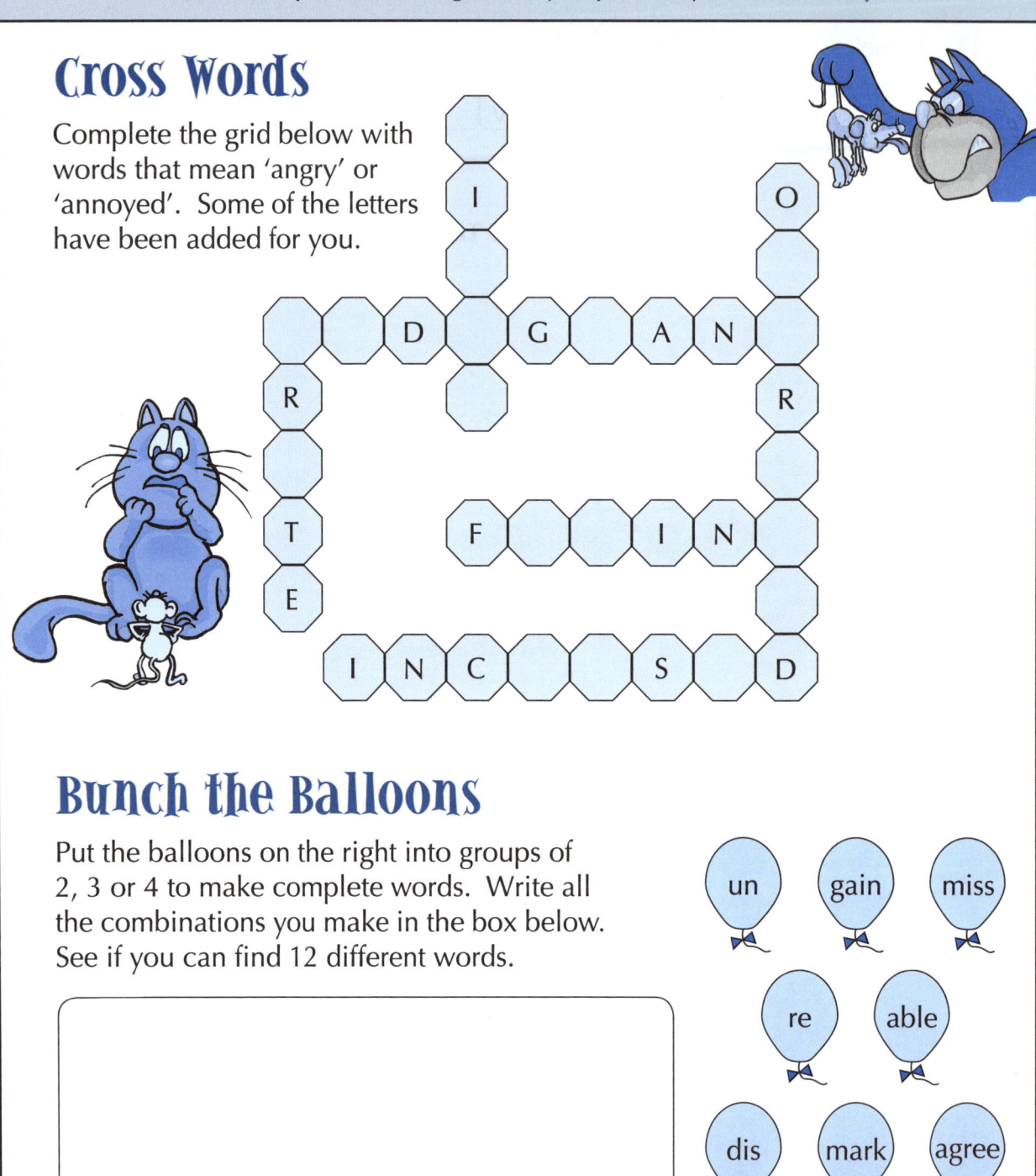

Answers

Test 1 — pages 2-4

1. yew
'yew' makes sense here — it is a type of tree, whereas 'ewe' is a female sheep.

2. missed
'missed' makes sense here — it the past tense of the verb 'to miss', whereas 'mist' means 'fog'.

3. foul
'foul' makes sense here — it means 'disgusting', whereas 'fowl' is the word for birds used for food.

4. boars
'boars' makes sense here — it is the word that refers to wild pigs, whereas 'boors' means 'rude people' and 'bores' means 'to make someone feel uninterested'.

5. scene
'scene' makes sense here — it is the word for part of a play, whereas 'seen' is from the verb 'to see'.

6. meddle
'meddle' makes sense here — it is the word that means 'to interfere', whereas 'medal' means 'a disc given as a prize'.

7. obtain
Both words mean 'get'.

8. intimidate
Both words mean 'bully'.

9. undesirable
Both words mean 'unwanted'.

10. apprehension
Both words mean 'fear'.

11. restore
Both words mean 're-establish'.

12. appropriate
Both words mean 'acceptable'.

13. credible
'implausible' can mean 'unbelievable', whereas 'credible' means 'believable'.

14. displease
'gratify' means 'to please', whereas 'displease' means 'to dissatisfy'.

15. inability
'capability' means 'ability', whereas 'inability' means 'lack of ability'.

16. granted
'withheld' means 'held back', whereas 'granted' means 'gave'.

17. unemotional
'expressive' means 'showing emotion', whereas 'unemotional' means 'not showing emotion'.

18. praise
'disparage' means 'to belittle', whereas 'praise' means 'to show admiration'.

19. INK
The complete word is SINKING.

20. LIE
The complete word is RELIEVED.

21. RAP
The complete word is SCRAPED.

22. RAT
The complete word is CRATES.

23. EAR
The complete word is SEARCH.

24. ARK
The complete word is MARKING.

25. ATE
The complete word is GREATER.

Test 2 — pages 5-6

1. endurable
The other three mean 'very difficult'.

2. scrutinise
The other three mean 'to watch over someone'.

3. haughty
The other three mean 'creative'.

4. capture
The other three mean 'to absorb someone's attention'.

5. director
The other three are performers.

6. hearty
'frail' means 'in poor health', whereas 'hearty' means 'healthy'.

7. meek
'overbearing' means 'bossy', whereas 'meek' means 'submissive'.

8. courteous
'rude' means 'impolite', whereas 'courteous' means 'polite'.

9. division
'unity' means 'being together', whereas 'division' means 'being separated'.

10. liberate
'arrest' means 'to take into custody', whereas 'liberate' means 'to set free'.

11. wane
'lessen' and 'wane' both mean 'decrease'.

12. dedicated
'zealous' and 'dedicated' both mean 'devoted to a goal'.

13. infirmity
'decrepitude' and 'infirmity' both mean 'weakness'.

14. develop
'formulate' and 'develop' both mean 'prepare'.

15. warily
'gingerly' and 'warily' both mean 'cautiously'.

16. charm
'captivate' and 'charm' both mean 'enchant'.

17. adequately
'sufficiently' and 'adequately' both mean 'enough'.

18. veil
'mask' and 'veil' both mean 'something that conceals the face'.

19. unique
'singular' and 'unique' both mean 'one of a kind'.

20. venture
'endeavour' and 'venture' both mean 'attempt'.

21. border
'border' can mean 'the edge of a piece of material' or 'the furthest edge'.

22. grate
'grate' can mean 'to break something down into small pieces' or 'to make an unpleasant sound'.

23. admit
'admit' can mean 'to allow inside' or 'to acknowledge something is true'.

24. uniform
'uniform' can mean 'clothing worn by people belonging to the same group' or 'unchanging'.

25. point
'point' can mean 'a specific location' or 'purpose'.

Puzzles 1 — page 7

Take Five
INFORM   repor**t** a**d**vise e**d**ucate **n**otify appris**e**
HORRIBLE   **v**ile ghast**l**y unpleasant repuls**v**e malicious
The unscrambled word is **accidental**.

Monkeying Around
Gerald's code words are **gullible**, **graceful** and **generous**.

Test 3 — pages 8-10

1. enterprise
'enterprise' is the only correctly spelled word that can be made.

2. uproar
'uproar' is the only correctly spelled word that can be made.

3. afterthought
'afterthought' is the only correctly spelled word that can be made.

4. bedrock
'bedrock' is the only correctly spelled word that can be made.

5. acceptable
'acceptable' is the only correctly spelled word that can be made.

6. heirloom
'heirloom' is the only correctly spelled word that can be made.

7. waylaid
'waylaid' is the only correctly spelled word that can be made.

8. discouraged
'heartened' means 'encouraged', whereas 'discouraged' means 'dispirited'.

9. kindled
'extinguished' means 'put out', whereas 'kindled' means 'awakened'.

10. turmoil
'tranquillity' means 'calm', whereas 'turmoil' means 'chaos'.

11. animosity
'friendship' means 'affection', whereas 'animosity' means 'hatred'.

12. compound
'mitigate' means 'lessen', whereas 'compound' means 'intensify'.

13. delightful
'odious' means 'horrible', whereas 'delightful' means 'pleasant'.

14. dubious
Both words mean 'doubtful'.

15. region
Both words mean 'an area'.

16. lasting
Both words mean 'enduring'.

17. exhibit
Both words mean 'to show'.

18. revelry
Both words mean 'festivity'.

19. outlaw
Both words mean 'a criminal'.

20. bone
A 'rib' is a 'bone' — ribs protect the heart and the lungs.

21. group
A 'swarm' is a 'group' — it is a large number of insects.

22. flower
An 'orchid' is a 'flower' — it is known for its unusual petals.

23. garment
A 'cardigan' is a 'garment' — 'garment' means 'piece of clothing'.

24. vegetable
An 'artichoke' is a 'vegetable' — it comes from a thistle plant.

25. sibling
A 'sister' is a 'sibling' — 'sibling' means 'brother or sister'.

Test 4 — pages 11-13

1. journey
The other three mean 'path'.

2. minister
The other three are monarchs.

3. welded
The other three mean 'interwoven'.

4. tower
The other three mean 'outdo'.

5. travel
The other three refer to places on a journey.

6. civil
The other three mean 'kind and affectionate'.

7. mane
'mane' makes sense here — it means 'hair on an animal's neck', whereas 'main' means 'the most important'.

8. drawer
'drawer' makes sense here — it is the word that means 'storage compartment', whereas 'draw' means 'to sketch'.

9. mourning
'mourning' makes sense here — it is the word that means 'a state of grief', whereas 'morning' means 'start of the day'.

10. profit
'profit' makes sense here — it is the word that means 'money gained', whereas 'prophet' means 'a seer'.

11. stationary
'stationary' makes sense here — it means 'not moving', whereas 'stationery' means 'office supplies'.

12. draft
'draft' makes sense here — it is the word that means 'first attempt', whereas 'draught' means 'a flow of cold air'.

13. mustered
'mustered' makes sense here — it is the word that means 'gathered', whereas 'mustard' is used to flavour food.

14. challenged
'challenged' makes sense here — 'questioned' and 'challenged' both mean 'disputed'.

15. astonishing
'astonishing' makes sense here — 'astounding' and 'astonishing' both mean 'incredible'.

16. escaped
'escaped' makes sense here — 'eluded' and 'escaped' both mean 'got away from'.

17. fragile
'fragile' makes sense here — 'delicate' and 'fragile' both mean 'dainty'.

18. ambition
'ambition' makes sense here — 'dream' and 'ambition' both mean 'goal'.

19. disastrous
'disastrous' makes sense here — 'catastrophic' and 'disastrous' both mean 'terrible'.

20. clarify
'clarify' means 'to make clear'.

21. amicable
'amicable' means 'friendly in nature'.

22. lethargy
'lethargy' means 'a lack of energy'.

23. disassemble
'disassemble' means 'to take apart'.

24. quell
'quell' means 'to end a disturbance'.

25. devious
'devious' means 'underhand and sneaky'.

Puzzles 2 — page 14

Alphabet Soup

3 letter words: e.g. **ace, arc, are, ark, can, car, con, ear, era, hen, her, nor, oak, oar, one, ore, ran, roe.**
4 letter words: e.g. **ache, arch, cake, cane, care, cone, core, cork, corn, each, hack, hake, hare, hear, hero, hone, horn, near, neck, once, orca, race, rack, rake, rank, rock.**
5 letter words: e.g. **acorn, canoe, choke, chore, crane, crank, creak, croak, crone, heron, ocean, ranch, reach.**
The 6 letter word is **anchor**.

Test 5 — pages 15-17

1. **timescale**
'timescale' is the only correctly spelled word that can be made.
2. **feedback**
'feedback' is the only correctly spelled word that can be made.
3. **snapshot**
'snapshot' is the only correctly spelled word that can be made.
4. **spellbound**
'spellbound' is the only correctly spelled word that can be made.
5. **minion**
'minion' is the only correctly spelled word that can be made.
6. **warrant**
'warrant' is the only correctly spelled word that can be made.
7. **instrument**
A 'cello' is an 'instrument' — it is a musical instrument.
8. **poem**
A 'limerick' is a 'poem' — it is a type of humorous poem.
9. **appliance**
A 'microwave' is an 'appliance' — an 'appliance' is a piece of equipment that is used for certain tasks.
10. **continent**
'Africa' is a 'continent' — a 'continent' is a big land mass.
11. **shellfish**
'lobster' is a 'shellfish' — 'shellfish' are a type of sea animal.
12. **fabric**
'chiffon' is a 'fabric' — it is a light material.
13. **de**test
'adore' means 'to love', whereas 'detest' means 'to hate'.
14. volu**ntary**
'mandatory' means 'required', whereas 'voluntary' means 'optional'.
15. en**ligh**ten
'mystify' means 'to confuse someone', whereas 'enlighten' means 'to make someone understand'.
16. dec**eit**fully
'sincerely' means 'honestly', whereas 'deceitfully' means 'dishonestly'.
17. con**clu**sion
'commencement' means 'the beginning of something', whereas 'conclusion' means 'the end of something'.
18. unfe**eling**
'compassionate' means 'showing care for others', whereas 'unfeeling' means 'not caring about the feelings of others'.
19. a**vera**ge
'extraordinary' means 'special', whereas 'average' means 'ordinary'.
20. **essential**
'essential' makes sense here — 'integral' and 'essential' both mean 'necessary'.
21. **drivel**
'drivel' makes sense here — 'nonsense' and 'drivel' both mean 'foolish talk'.
22. **sizeable**
'sizeable' makes sense here — 'substantial' and 'sizeable' both mean 'large'.
23. **implored**
'implored' makes sense here — 'begged' and 'implored' both mean 'pleaded'.
24. **apparent**
'apparent' makes sense here — 'evident' and 'apparent' both mean 'clear'.
25. **ramshackle**
'ramshackle' makes sense here — 'dilapidated' and 'ramshackle' both mean 'run down'.

Test 6 — pages 18-19

1. **sundial**
'sundial' is the only correctly spelled word that can be made.
2. **reinvest**
'reinvest' is the only correctly spelled word that can be made.
3. **justice**
'justice' is the only correctly spelled word that can be made.
4. **target**
'target' is the only correctly spelled word that can be made.
5. **watertight**
'watertight' is the only correctly spelled word that can be made.
6. **benign**
'benign' means 'mild in nature'.
7. **lull**
'lull' means 'a period of calm'.
8. **circumnavigate**
'circumnavigate' means 'to go around'.
9. **grit**
'grit' means 'firmness of character'.
10. **parable**
'parable' means 'a story with a moral'.
11. **rationally**
'illogically' means 'senselessly', whereas 'rationally' means 'sensibly'.
12. **faultless**
'defective' means 'flawed', whereas 'faultless' means 'perfect'.

13. recede
'advance' means 'move forwards', whereas 'recede' means 'move backwards'.

14. order
'mayhem' means 'chaos', whereas 'order' means 'organisation'.

15. pollute
'cleanse' means 'to clean', whereas 'pollute' means 'to contaminate'.

16. supple
'rigid' means 'stiff', whereas 'supple' means 'flexible'.

17. radically
'moderately' means 'somewhat', whereas 'radically' means 'completely'.

18. convince
'dissuade' means 'to talk someone out of something', whereas 'convince' means 'to talk someone into something'.

19. furious
'placid' means 'calm', whereas 'furious' means 'very angry'.

20. contrast
'resemblance' means 'similarity', whereas 'contrast' means 'difference'.

21. of*fend*er
Both words mean 'a criminal'.

22. de*cis*ion
Both words mean 'a final judgement'.

23. m*emor*y
Both words mean 'something that is remembered'.

24. rela*t*ed
Both words mean 'connected to'.

25. d*o*cile
Both words mean 'meek'.

Test 7 — pages 20-22

1. event
Both words mean 'a happening'.

2. silky
Both words mean 'smooth'.

3. conscientiously
Both words mean 'in a careful way'.

4. unsound
Both words mean 'faulty'.

5. rise
Both words mean 'to climb'.

6. scamper
Both words mean 'to move in a hurry'.

7. acorn
The other three are types of tree.

8. decay
The other three mean 'to break apart'.

9. vapour
The other three are processes in turning water into a solid, liquid or gas.

10. tunnel
The other three are above the ground.

11. standard
The other three mean 'strange'.

12. composed
The other three mean 'very happy'.

13. impractical
'viable' can mean 'realistic', whereas 'impractical' can mean 'unrealistic'.

14. dullness
'sheen' means 'shine', whereas 'dullness' means 'drabness'.

15. biased
'objective' means 'fair', whereas 'biased' means 'unfairly prejudiced'.

16. conflict
'accord' means 'agreement', whereas 'conflict' means 'disagreement'.

17. denied
'conceded' means 'admitted', whereas 'denied' means 'refused to admit'.

18. exceptional
'mediocre' means 'average', whereas 'exceptional' means 'very special'.

19. subject
'subject' can mean 'the thing being discussed' or 'likely to be affected by something'.

20. bore
'bore' can mean 'to make a hole in something' or 'something tiresome'.

21. term
'term' can mean 'a time period' or 'a word or phrase that describes a concept'.

22. stamp
'stamp' can mean 'to bring your foot to the ground' or 'to make a mark using a stamp'.

23. scale
'scale' can mean 'to climb something steep' or 'a range of values'.

24. balance
'balance' can mean 'to make equal' or 'a state in which different elements are equal'.

25. passage
'passage' can mean 'a journey by sea or air' or 'a narrow pathway'.

Puzzles 3 — page 23

Write It Right
1. **plane** and **plain**
2. **practice** and **practise**
3. **sew** and **sow**

Rory's Story
pale — pile — mile — milk — silk — sulk

Test 8 — pages 24-26

1. **LOT**
The complete word is BLOTCH.

2. **APE**
The complete word is SHAPED.

3. **LAD**
The complete word is BLADES.

4. **LAW**
The complete word is FLAWED.

5. **LOW**
The complete word is BLOWING.

6. **FIN**
The complete word is DEFINED.

7. **beverage**
'coffee' is a 'beverage' — 'beverage' means 'drink'.

8. **direction**
'west' is a 'direction' — it is a compass point.

9. **cutlery**
A 'spoon' is a piece of 'cutlery' — 'cutlery' includes spoons, knives and forks.

10. **competition**
A 'tournament' is a 'competition' — it is a series of matches.

11. **fuel**
'petrol' is a 'fuel' — a 'fuel' is an energy source.

12. **word**
An 'adjective' is a 'word' — it is a describing word.

13. **stationery**
A 'staple' is a piece of 'stationery' — 'stationery' describes office supplies such as pens and paper.

14. **mo**men**tous**
'insignificant' means 'unimportant', whereas 'momentous' means 'very important'.

15. **par**do**n**
'punish' means 'to penalise', whereas 'pardon' means 'to forgive'.

16. **serious**
'flippant' means 'not being serious', whereas 'serious' means 'acting earnestly'.

17. **darken**
'illuminate' means 'to light up', whereas 'darken' means 'to make dark'.

18. **denial**
'acceptance' means 'believing in the truth of something', whereas 'denial' means 'not believing something is true'.

19. **arrogance**
'humility' means 'modesty', whereas 'arrogance' means 'pride'.

20. **oppose**
Both words mean 'to differ in opinion'.

21. **disdain**
Both words mean 'a dislike of or aversion to something'.

22. **continual**
Both words mean 'continuing without a break'.

23. **vigorously**
Both words mean 'energetically'.

24. **assortment**
Both words mean 'a mixture of types'.

25. **merit**
Both words mean 'a positive quality'.

Test 9 — pages 27-29

1. **ring**
'ring' makes sense here — it is the word that can mean 'a space for boxing', whereas 'wring' means 'twist'.

2. **freeze**
'freeze' makes sense here — it is the word that means 'make cold', whereas 'frees' means 'lets go' and 'frieze' is a type of decoration.

3. **farther**
'farther' makes sense here — it is the word that describes distance, whereas 'father' means 'parent'.

4. **dessert**
'dessert' makes sense here — it is the word that means 'pudding', whereas 'desert' means 'to abandon'.

5. **led**
'led' makes sense here — it is the past tense of 'to lead', whereas 'lead' is a type of metal.

6. **descent**
'descent' makes sense here — it is the word that means 'going down', whereas 'dissent' means 'disagreement'.

7. **transmit**
'transmit' means 'to send out'.

8. **affinity**
'affinity' means 'a liking for'.

9. **thrive**
'thrive' means 'to grow strongly'.

10. macabre
'macabre' means 'related to death'.

11. forfeit
'forfeit' means 'to give up'.

12. disclose
'disclose' means 'to make known'.

13. seclusion
Both words mean 'separation from others'.

14. severe
Both words mean 'harsh'.

15. teamwor**k**
Both words mean 'cooperation'.

16. specify
Both words mean 'indicate the limits of something'.

17. rural
Both words mean 'of the countryside'.

18. commen**t**
Both words mean 'mention'.

19. identify
Both words mean 'to recognise precisely'.

20. lauded
'condemned' means 'criticised', whereas 'lauded' means 'praised'.

21. unintelligible
'comprehensible' means 'understandable', whereas 'unintelligible' means 'not understandable'.

22. apathy
'enthusiasm' means 'eagerness', whereas 'apathy' means 'disinterest'.

23. exposed
'concealed' means 'hidden', whereas 'exposed' means 'uncovered'.

24. susceptible
'immune' means 'unaffected by', whereas 'susceptible' means 'open to'.

25. cheery
'sullen' means 'grumpy', whereas 'cheery' means 'happy'.

Test 10 — pages 30-31

1. pick
'pick' can mean 'to gather flowers, fruits or vegetables' or 'the chosen option'.

2. litter
'litter' can mean 'rubbish' or 'an animal's young that are born at the same time'.

3. hamper
'hamper' can mean 'a basket containing food' or 'to block'.

4. hunch
'hunch' can mean 'to bend' or 'a feeling based on instinct'.

5. field
'field' can mean 'an area of study' or 'an area of land'.

6. brainwash
'brainwash' is the only correctly spelled word that can be made.

7. headlight
'headlight' is the only correctly spelled word that can be made.

8. viewpoint
'viewpoint' is the only correctly spelled word that can be made.

9. forever
'forever' is the only correctly spelled word that can be made.

10. changeable
'changeable' is the only correctly spelled word that can be made.

11. conspire
'collude' and 'conspire' both mean 'plot'.

12. uninspiring
'lacklustre' and 'uninspiring' both mean 'dull'.

13. bargain
'negotiate' and 'bargain' both mean 'to haggle'.

14. skilful
'adept' and 'skilful' both mean 'accomplished'.

15. significance
'magnitude' and 'significance' both mean 'importance'.

16. berate
'chide' and 'berate' both mean 'to criticise'.

17. daring
'intrepid' and 'daring' both mean 'brave'.

18. assess
'appraise' and 'assess' both mean 'to evaluate'.

19. paradise
'utopia' and 'paradise' both mean 'heaven'.

20. veneer
'appearance' and 'veneer' both mean 'an outward show'.

21. com**ply**
'rebel' means 'to not obey', whereas 'comply' means 'to obey'.

22. dis**appro**val
'favour' means 'approval', whereas 'disapproval' can mean 'criticism'.

23. **rel**ease
'confine' means 'to imprison', whereas 'release' means 'to free'.

24. ec**onom**ical
'wasteful' means 'careless with resources', whereas 'economical' means 'careful with resources'.

25. dis**loyal**ty
'fidelity' means 'loyalty', whereas 'disloyalty' means 'lack of loyalty'.

Puzzles 4 — page 32

Puzzling Prefixes
re — connect — reconnect
in — secure — insecure
un — marked — unmarked
dis — satisfy — dissatisfy

Twin-onyms

Test 11 — pages 33-35

1. **grown**
'grown' makes sense here — it is the past tense of the verb 'to grow', whereas 'groan' means 'to moan'.

2. **guest**
'guest' makes sense here — it is the word that means 'visitor', whereas 'guessed' is the past tense of the verb 'to guess'.

3. **chord**
'chord' makes sense here — it is the word that means 'a group of musical notes', whereas 'cored' means 'cut out the centre' and 'cord' means 'rope'.

4. **ball**
'ball' makes sense here — it is the word that means 'a dance', whereas 'bawl' means 'to cry'.

5. **grate**
'grate' makes sense here — it is the word that describes part of a fireplace, whereas 'great' means 'very good'.

6. **stairs**
'stairs' makes sense here — it is the word that means 'steps', whereas 'stares' means 'looks'.

7. **form**
'form' can mean 'the design of something' or 'to assemble'.

8. **fray**
'fray' can mean 'a fight' or 'to come apart'.

9. **current**
'current' can mean 'the flow of something' or 'of the present time'.

10. **clip**
'clip' can mean 'to cut short' or 'a small part'.

11. **share**
'share' can mean 'a part of a larger amount' or 'to divide up'.

12. **arrange**
'arrange' can mean 'to put in order' or 'to make plans'.

13. **penalise**
'reward' means 'to honour', whereas 'penalise' means 'to punish'.

14. **fleeting**
'eternal' means 'lasting forever', whereas 'fleeting' means 'brief'.

15. **yield**
'resist' means 'to struggle against', whereas 'yield' means 'to give in'.

16. **inhabited**
'deserted' means 'not inhabited', whereas 'inhabited' means 'lived in'.

17. **descendant**
'ancestor' means 'a person you're descended from', whereas 'descendant' means 'a person descended from you'.

18. **hushed**
'raucous' means 'loud', whereas 'hushed' means 'quiet'.

19. **frequently**
'seldom' means 'rarely', whereas 'frequently' means 'often'.

20. **connived**
'connived' makes sense here — 'plotted' and 'connived' both mean 'conspired'.

21. **adamant**
'adamant' makes sense here — 'determined' and 'adamant' both mean 'insistent'.

22. **acclaimed**
'acclaimed' makes sense here — 'noted' and 'acclaimed' both mean 'renowned'.

23. **honoured**
'honoured' makes sense here — 'privileged' and 'honoured' both mean 'favoured'.

24. **inquisition**
'inquisition' makes sense here — 'interrogation' and 'inquisition' both mean 'examination by questioning'.

25. **prohibited**
'prohibited' makes sense here — 'forbidden' and 'prohibited' both mean 'banned'.

Test 12 — pages 36-38

1. ILL
The complete word is HILLIEST.

2. EAR
The complete word is DEARLY.

3. ART
The complete word is DARTED.

4. BIN
The complete word is CABINS.

5. ASH
The complete word is SASHES.

6. prudence
'folly' means 'foolishness', whereas 'prudence' means 'caution'.

7. accepted
'declined' means 'refused', whereas 'accepted' means 'consented to'.

8. artificial
'genuine' means 'real', whereas 'artificial' means 'fake'.

9. ridiculous
'sensible' means 'rational', whereas 'ridiculous' means 'foolish'.

10. undetected
'perceived' means 'sensed', whereas 'undetected' means 'not sensed'.

11. obstruct
'unblock' means 'to clear', whereas 'obstruct' means 'to block'.

12. alienate
'include' means 'to make someone part of something', whereas 'alienate' means 'to make someone feel unwanted'.

13. assertive
'submissive' means 'meek', whereas 'assertive' means 'forceful'.

14. excess
'dearth' means 'lack of', whereas 'excess' means 'too much of'.

15. calm
'agitation' means 'turmoil', whereas 'calm' means 'peace'.

16. recommend
Both words mean 'to propose someone for a position'.

17. educated
Both words mean 'knowledgeable'.

18. escort
Both words mean 'to guide'.

19. messenger
Both words refer to someone who transports goods or messages.

20. authority
Both words mean 'control over others'.

21. coat
An 'anorak' is a 'coat' — it is a waterproof jacket.

22. goddess
'Venus' is a 'goddess' — she is the Roman goddess of love.

23. currency
'Euro' is a 'currency' — 'currency' is the money that's used in a certain place.

24. performance
An 'encore' is a 'performance' — it is an additional performance at the end of show.

25. carving
A 'sculpture' is a 'carving' — it is a type of art made by carving materials such as stone and wood.

Test 13 — pages 39-41

1. casual
'formal' means 'smart or proper', whereas 'casual' means 'relaxed'.

2. caution
'recklessness' means 'carelessness', whereas 'caution' means 'care'.

3. youth
'maturity' means 'adulthood', whereas 'youth' means 'early life'.

4. unwise
'advisable' means 'sensible', whereas 'unwise' means 'foolish'.

5. commotion
'calmness' means 'peace', whereas 'commotion' means 'uproar'.

6. stuffy
'airy' means 'well-aired', whereas 'stuffy' means 'lacking fresh air'.

7. wreck
'construct' means 'to build', whereas 'wreck' means 'to destroy'.

8. basic
The other three mean 'blunt in approach'.

9. spelling
The other three are parts of a sentence.

10. needle
The other three mean 'to sew'.

11. entrust
The other three mean 'to prove innocent'.

12. excusably
The other three mean 'in a believable way'.

13. duke
The other three are titles for women.

14. intriguing
'intriguing' makes sense here — 'fascinating' and 'intriguing' both mean 'interesting'.

15. majestic
'majestic' makes sense here — 'magnificent' and 'majestic' both mean 'impressive'.

16. laborious
'laborious' makes sense here — 'gruelling' and 'laborious' and both mean 'strenuous'.

17. scolded
'scolded' makes sense here — 'chastised' and 'scolded' both mean 'told off'.

18. abominably
'abominably' makes sense here — 'despicably' and 'abominably' both mean 'very badly'.

19. languished
'languished' makes sense here — 'withered' and 'languished' both mean 'deteriorated'.

20. permeate
'permeate' means 'to spread through'.

21. unequivocal
'unequivocal' means 'leaving no doubt'.

22. tactical
'tactical' means 'using strategy'.

23. dialect
'dialect' means 'a local language'.

24. creep
'creep' means 'to move stealthily'.

25. altitude
'altitude' can mean 'great height'.

Puzzles 5 — page 42

Befuddled Basketballs
Top rack: lonely, **solitary**, **individual**, **person**.
Bottom rack: solemn, **sombre**, dull, **tedious**.

Bird is the Word
~~willing~~ — wing
~~fully~~ — fly
~~promisingly~~ — sing
~~sneakiest~~ — nest

Test 14 — pages 43-45

1. ANT
The complete word is DECANTS.

2. END
The complete word is GENDER.

3. RIP
The complete word is UNRIPE.

4. NOR
The complete word is SNORTED.

5. SET
The complete word is RESETS.

6. RAT
The complete word is GRATED.

7. possibility
'certainty' means 'something that is sure to happen', whereas 'possibility' means 'something that might happen'.

8. charitable
'miserly' means 'reluctant to spend money', whereas 'charitable' means 'willing to give'.

9. deter
'incite' means 'encourage', whereas 'deter' means 'discourage'.

10. crude
'elegant' means 'refined', whereas 'crude' means 'unrefined'.

11. hopefulness
'despondency' means 'lacking hope', whereas 'hopefulness' means 'optimism'.

12. authorise
'deny' means 'to refuse to allow', whereas 'authorise' means 'to allow'.

13. overflow
'overflow' is the only correctly spelled word that can be made.

14. nothing
'nothing' is the only correctly spelled word that can be made.

15. setback
'setback' is the only correctly spelled word that can be made.

16. heartier
'heartier' is the only correctly spelled word that can be made.

17. putrid
'putrid' is the only correctly spelled word that can be made.

18. deadline
'deadline' is the only correctly spelled word that can be made.

19. assignment
Both words mean 'a job'.

20. unstable
Both words mean 'shaky'.

21. c**r**ave
Both words mean 'to desire'.

22. dreame**r**
Both words mean 'someone who wants things to be better'.

23. mo**r**tify
Both words mean 'to embarrass'.

24. pat**r**onising
Both words mean 'looks down on others'.

25. st**r**ive
Both words mean 'to try hard'.

Test 15 — pages 46-48

1. abundant
Both words mean 'ample'.

2. conceit
Both words mean 'arrogance'.

3. terminate
Both words mean 'to finish'.

4. authentic
Both words mean 'genuine'.

5. inconsistently
Both words mean 'irregularly'.

6. particular
Both words mean 'choosy'.

7. confiscate
The other three mean 'to take unlawfully'.

8. ivory
The other three are shades of blue.

9. routine
The other three can mean 'a religious ritual'.

10. illustration
The other three refer to people who create art.

11. hereditary
The other three mean 'old'.

12. address
The other three are areas of land.

13. emotion
'elation' is an 'emotion' — it is a feeling of great happiness.

14. pilot
An 'aviator' is a 'pilot' — it is someone who flies aircraft.

15. tool
A 'wrench' is a 'tool' — it is used for turning nuts and bolts.

16. cup
A 'chalice' is a 'cup' — it is a large cup or goblet.

17. spice
'paprika' is a 'spice' — a 'spice' is something that is used to flavour food.

18. citrus
'lemon' is a 'citrus' — citrus fruits include lemons, limes and oranges.

19. vitality
Both words mean 'power and vigour'.

20. adve**r**tise
Both words mean 'to publicise'.

21. col**ossal**
Both words mean 'huge'.

22. **m**ission
Both words mean 'a task'.

23. un**k**empt
Both words mean 'scruffy'.

24. mimi**c**
Both words mean 'to copy'.

25. d**e**vout
Both words mean 'passionate about something'.

Test 16 — pages 49-51

1. ornate
'ornate' means 'elaborately decorated'.

2. review
'review' means 'an official assessment'.

3. droll
'droll' means 'causing amusement'.

4. dexterous
'dexterous' means 'possessing skill'.

5. spectacle
'spectacle' means 'a great display'.

6. inert
'inert' means 'unable to move'.

7. backdrop
'backdrop' is the only correctly spelled word that can be made.

8. supernatural
'supernatural' is the only correctly spelled word that can be made.

9. commonplace
'commonplace' is the only correctly spelled word that can be made.

10. meanwhile
'meanwhile' is the only correctly spelled word that can be made.

11. browsing
'browsing' is the only correctly spelled word that can be made.

12. **feather**
'feather' is the only correctly spelled word that can be made.

13. si**lence**
'clamour' means 'noise', whereas 'silence' means 'quiet'.

14. per**seve**re
'quit' means 'give up', whereas 'persevere' means 'keep going'.

15. indi**v**idual
'universal' means 'very widely occurring', whereas 'individual' means 'occurring only once'.

16. ig**nore**
'observe' means 'to pay attention to', whereas 'ignore' means 'to take no notice of'.

17. ex**pe**rt
'inexperienced' means 'new to something', whereas 'expert' means 'very experienced'.

18. vict**or**ious
'defeated' means 'beaten', whereas 'victorious' means 'having won'.

19. imp**ossib**le
'achievable' means 'possible', whereas 'impossible' means 'can't be done'.

20. **eventful**
'monotonous' means 'dull', whereas 'eventful' means 'exciting'.

21. **finite**
'boundless' means 'endless', whereas 'finite' means 'limited'.

22. **exaggerated**
'understated' means 'downplayed', whereas 'exaggerated' means 'overemphasised'.

23. **curtailed**
'lengthened' means 'made longer', whereas 'curtailed' means 'cut short'.

24. **submission**
'rebellion' means 'disobedience', whereas 'submission' means 'compliance'.

25. **weakened**
'fortified' means 'made stronger', whereas 'weakened' means 'made less strong'.

Puzzles 6 — page 52

Rhyme Time
veri**fiable**   un**deniable**   **reliable**   jus**tifiable**

Target Practice
The six new words are:
dash**board** and white**board**
play**ground** and under**ground**
other**wise** and like**wise**

Test 17 — pages 53-54

1. **piece**
'piece' makes sense here — it is the word that means 'part', whereas 'peace' means 'harmony'.

2. **effect**
'effect' makes sense here — it is the word that means 'result', whereas 'affect' means 'to influence'.

3. **heal**
'heal' makes sense here — it is the word that means 'get better', whereas 'heel' is part of a foot and 'he'll' means 'he will'.

4. **whole**
'whole' makes sense here — it is the word that means 'entire', whereas 'hole' means 'an opening'.

5. **hoarse**
'hoarse' makes sense here — it is the word that means 'croaky', whereas 'horse' is an animal.

6. **lower**
'lower' can mean 'lower in status' or 'to make smaller'.

7. **associate**
'associate' can mean 'to make a connection between two things' or 'a person you work with'.

8. **accept**
'accept' can mean 'to recognise something is true' or 'to approve of something'.

9. **character**
'character' can mean 'a written symbol' or 'identity'.

10. **discount**
'discount' can mean 'to ignore' or 'a lower price'.

11. **significant**
'meaningless' means 'unimportant', whereas 'significant' means 'important'.

12. **resolutely**
'tentatively' means 'hesitantly', whereas 'resolutely' means 'determinedly'.

13. **expand**
'abbreviate' means 'shorten', whereas 'expand' means 'enlarge'.

14. **praise**
'criticism' means 'disapproval', whereas 'praise' means 'a compliment'.

15. **repellent**
'pleasant' means 'pleasing', whereas 'repellent' means 'disgusting'.

16. **hostility**
'friendliness' means 'warmth and affection', whereas 'hostility' means 'enmity'.

17. **assemble**
'dismantle' means 'take apart', whereas 'assemble' means 'put together'.

18. **protrud**ing
'sunken' means 'buried', whereas 'protruding' means 'sticking out'.

19. **subt**ly
'bluntly' means 'in a direct way', whereas 'subtly' means 'delicately'.

20. **feeb**le
'vigorous' means 'powerful', whereas 'feeble' means 'weak'.

21. **sty**le
Both words mean 'a talent for fashion'.

22. **tor**rent
Both words mean 'a heavy flow'.

23. **in**te**rrup**tion
Both words mean 'a break'.

24. **thea**trical
Both words mean 'exaggerated'.

25. **lu**ke**wa**rm
Both words mean 'slightly warm'.

Test 18 — pages 55-57

1. **ICE**
The complete word is PRICES.

2. **APP**
The complete word is TAPPING.

3. **AND**
The complete word is BRANDS.

4. **IRE**
The complete word is SIRENS.

5. **USE**
The complete word is DEFUSES.

6. **VIE**
The complete word is ENVIES.

7. **wizardry**
The other three refer to people with magical powers.

8. **erased**
The other three mean 'damaged or made dirty'.

9. **resentful**
The other three mean 'unfriendly'.

10. **armed**
The other three mean 'guarded'.

11. **bashful**
The other three mean 'obedient'.

12. **injury**
The other three mean 'catastrophe'.

13. ac**knowl**edge
'disclaim' means 'to deny', whereas 'acknowledge' means 'to accept'.

14. de**duc**tion
'increase' means 'addition', whereas 'deduction' means 'subtraction'.

15. c**lum**sy
'coordinated' means 'all parts acting together', whereas 'clumsy' means 'awkward in movement'.

16. **timi**d
'courageous' means 'brave', whereas 'timid' means 'nervous'.

17. a**ggr**avate
'appease' means 'soothe', whereas 'aggravate' means 'annoy'.

18. ha**rmle**ss
'dangerous' means 'harmful', whereas 'harmless' means 'not dangerous'.

19. neg**ligen**ce
'care' means 'attention to detail', whereas 'negligence' means 'lack of care'.

20. **dire**
Both words mean 'terrible'.

21. **appreciative**
Both words mean 'thankful'.

22. **communicate**
Both words can mean 'to exchange ideas with other people'.

23. **animated**
Both words mean 'energetic'.

24. **notion**
Both words mean 'an idea'.

25. **strain**
Both words mean 'to elongate'.

Test 19 — pages 58-59

1. **dimin**ish
'enlarge' means 'to grow', whereas 'diminish' means 'to decrease'.

2. **safe**ty
'peril' means 'danger', whereas 'safety' means 'protected from danger'.

3. g**loo**m
'cheer' means 'joy', whereas 'gloom' means 'unhappiness'.

4. **no**tic**ea**ble
'inconspicuous' means 'not obvious', whereas 'noticeable' means 'attracting attention'.

5. **tr**us**t**ing
'doubting' means 'questioning', whereas 'trusting' means 'believing'.

6. beat
'beat' can mean 'the rhythm in music' or 'to defeat'.

7. blossom
'blossom' can mean 'flowers' or 'to develop in a positive way'.

8. bound
'bound' can mean 'to leap' or 'obliged to do something'.

9. brief
'brief' can mean 'short' or 'to explain something in preparation for a task'.

10. challenge
'challenge' can mean 'a situation that tests your abilities' or 'to dispute something'.

11. proverb
'proverb' means 'a common saying'.

12. spry
'spry' means 'full of energy'.

13. wily
'wily' means 'crafty in nature'.

14. smirk
'smirk' means 'a smug smile'.

15. wrench
'wrench' means 'to pull hard'.

16. eclectic
'diverse' and 'eclectic' both mean 'varied'.

17. affirm
'insist' and 'affirm' both mean 'to stand by a view'.

18. absorb
'incorporate' and 'absorb' both mean 'to take in'.

19. calling
'vocation' and 'calling' both mean 'a chosen career'.

20. gift
'bequest' and 'gift' both mean 'a present'.

21. control
'operate' and 'control' both mean 'to be in charge of'.

22. portrayal
'depiction' and 'portrayal' both mean 'a representation'.

23. ludicrous
'farcical' and 'ludicrous' both mean 'absurd'.

24. perceive
'notice' and 'perceive' both mean 'to detect'.

25. dilemma
'quandary' and 'dilemma' both mean 'a puzzle or difficulty'.

Puzzles 7 — page 60

Witch Words

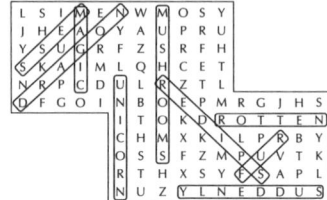

The missing words are: **mess**, **unicorn**, **fur**, **spider**, **dragon**, **mushrooms**, **rotten**, **magic**, **suddenly**.

Test 20 — pages 61-63

1. depart
'linger' means 'to remain', whereas 'depart' means 'to leave'.

2. increase
'deplete' can mean 'diminish', whereas 'increase' means 'grow'.

3. secluded
'open' means 'exposed', whereas 'secluded' means 'sheltered'.

4. dishonesty
'integrity' means 'being honest', whereas 'dishonesty' means 'not being honest'.

5. peripheral
'central' means 'in the middle', whereas 'peripheral' means 'on the edge'.

6. approximately
'precisely' means 'exactly', whereas 'approximately' means 'roughly'.

7. suite
'suite' makes sense here — it is the word that means 'set of rooms', whereas 'sweet' means 'sugary'.

8. banned
'banned' makes sense here — it is the word that means 'forbidden', whereas 'band' means 'musical group'.

9. aisle
'aisle' makes sense here — it is the word that means 'corridor', whereas 'isle' means 'island'.

10. due
'due' makes sense here — it is the word that means 'expected', whereas 'dew' means 'drops of water'.

11. sore
'sore' makes sense here — it is the word that means 'painful', whereas 'soar' means 'to fly', and 'saw' is a tool for cutting.

12. role
'role' makes sense here — it is the word that means 'a part', whereas 'roll' means 'to turn'.

13. nostal**gic**
Both words can mean 'feeling a longing for the past'.

Answers

14. rivalr**y**
Both words mean 'a contest'.

15. pitiful
Both words mean 'very small and weak'.

16. erupt
Both words mean 'to burst'.

17. rupture
Both words mean 'split'.

18. gifted
Both words mean 'naturally good at something'.

19. suggest
Both words mean 'to hint'.

20. LIE
The complete word is ALLIES.

21. PIN
The complete word is UNPINS.

22. CUR
The complete word is INCURS.

23. APP
The complete word is RAPPER.

24. OWE
The complete word is TOWERS.

25. PAR
The complete word is PREPARED.

Test 21 — pages 64-66

1. waver
'decide' means 'to make a decision', whereas 'waver' means 'to be indecisive'.

2. extreme
'mild' means 'not intense', whereas 'extreme' means 'intense'.

3. refined
'uncouth' means 'lacking manners', whereas 'refined' means 'civilised'.

4. regularity
'variation' means 'difference', whereas 'regularity' means 'consistency'.

5. embrace
'renounce' means 'to reject', whereas 'embrace' means 'to welcome'.

6. modest
'smug' means 'having too much pride in yourself', whereas 'modest' means 'free from pride'.

7. refuge
Both words mean 'a shelter'.

8. profitable
Both words mean 'money-making'.

9. burden
Both words mean 'a responsibility'.

10. advo**c**ate
Both words mean 'to be in favour of something'.

11. fluke
Both words mean 'chance'.

12. focus
Both words mean 'to pay attention to'.

13. jovial
Both words mean 'happy'.

14. aristocrat
An 'earl' is an 'aristocrat' — an 'aristocrat' is a noble.

15. organ
A 'kidney' is an 'organ' — an 'organ' is a part of the body that has a specific purpose.

16. boat
A 'vessel' is a 'boat' — 'vessel' is another word for a ship or boat.

17. mammal
A 'rodent' is a 'mammal' — 'rodent' is used to describe small mammals like mice and rats.

18. cheese
'Stilton' is a 'cheese' — it is a British cheese.

19. offence
'fraud' is an 'offence' — 'offence' can mean 'crime'.

20. abhor
'abhor' means 'to strongly hate'.

21. insipid
'insipid' means 'weak in flavour'.

22. alleviate
'alleviate' means 'to make milder'.

23. facade
'facade' means 'a false appearance'.

24. prattle
'prattle' means 'to talk at length'.

25. slacken
'slacken' means 'to make loose'.

Test 22 — 67-69

1. **resigned**
   The other three mean 'sacked'.
2. **methodology**
   The other three mean 'methodical'.
3. **clairvoyant**
   The other three mean 'a vision of the future'.
4. **argument**
   The other three are physical fights.
5. **prior**
   The other three mean 'coming after'.
6. **bronze**
   The other three are precious stones.
7. **supply**
   'supply' is the only correctly spelled word that can be made.
8. **worthwhile**
   'worthwhile' is the only correctly spelled word that can be made.
9. **underestimate**
   'underestimate' is the only correctly spelled word that can be made.
10. **primate**
    'primate' is the only correctly spelled word that can be made.
11. **threadbare**
    'threadbare' is the only correctly spelled word that can be made.
12. **thunderstruck**
    'thunderstruck' is the only correctly spelled word that can be made.
13. **fish**
    'herring' is a 'fish' — it is a small fish found in coastal waters.
14. **song**
    A 'hymn' is a 'song' — it is a religious song of praise.
15. **street**
    A 'boulevard' is a 'street' — a 'boulevard' is a wide street, often lined with trees.
16. **umbrella**
    A 'parasol' is an 'umbrella' — it is used to give protection from the sun.
17. **settlement**
    A 'hamlet' is a 'settlement' — it is smaller than a village.
18. **pen**
    A 'quill' is a 'pen' — it is a made from a feather.
19. **language**
    'slang' is a type of 'language' — 'slang' uses very informal words and phrases.
20. **stupidity**
    'sagacity' means 'wisdom', whereas 'stupidity' means 'foolishness'.
21. **attentive**
    'inconsiderate' means 'insensitive', whereas 'attentive' means 'thoughtful'.
22. **disturbed**
    'soothed' means 'calmed', whereas 'disturbed' means 'upset'.
23. **halting**
    'initiating' means 'starting', whereas 'halting' means 'stopping'.
24. **supercilious**
    'humble' means 'modest', whereas 'supercilious' means 'arrogant'.
25. **frailty**
    'frailty' means 'weakness', whereas 'strength' means 'power'.

Puzzles 8 — page 70

Crack the Code
THE TREASURE IS BENEATH THE SHED

Mine Mayhem
The words are: **rest**ricted, **em**ployees, im**port**ant, **hea**lth, mea**sure**s, env**iron**ment, **every**one, **conc**erns.

Test 23 — pages 71-73

1. **clause**
   'clause' makes sense here — it is the word that describes part of a sentence, whereas 'claws' are animals' nails.
2. **heir**
   'heir' makes sense here — it is the word that means 'person who inherits', whereas 'air' means 'atmosphere'.
3. **dual**
   'dual' makes sense here — it is the word that means 'double', whereas 'duel' means 'a fight'.
4. **seam**
   'seam' makes sense here — it is the word that means 'a join in fabric', whereas 'seem' means 'to appear'.
5. **break**
   'break' makes sense here — it is the word that means 'stop an action', whereas 'brake' means 'to slow down'.
6. **pier**
   'pier' makes sense here — it is the word that means 'platform leading into the sea', whereas 'peer' means 'to look'.
7. **gauge**
   'gauge' can mean 'an instrument of measurement' or 'to assess'.
8. **straight**
   'straight' can mean 'honest' or 'not curved'.

9. crane
'crane' can mean 'to stretch in order to see something' or 'a tall machine for lifting objects'.

10. type
'type' can mean 'a group of things with common characteristics' or 'characters or letters'.

11. splinter
'splinter' can mean 'to break into pieces' or 'a small, thin piece of something'.

12. square
'square' can mean 'straight and equal' or 'an area that has four sides'.

13. intentional
'inadvertent' means 'accidental', whereas 'intentional' means 'deliberate'.

14. defy
'obey' means 'to follow orders', whereas 'defy' means 'to go against orders'.

15. confirm
'disprove' means 'to prove false', whereas 'confirm' means 'to show that something is correct'.

16. organised
'disarranged' means 'disordered', whereas 'organised' means 'put in order'.

17. harmony
'disagreement' means 'conflict', whereas 'harmony' means 'agreement'.

18. regular
'sporadic' means 'happens occasionally', whereas 'regular' means 'happens consistently'.

19. mockery
'mockery' makes sense here — 'derision' and 'mockery' both mean 'ridicule'.

20. flamboyant
'flamboyant' makes sense here — 'ostentatious' and 'flamboyant' both mean 'extravagant'.

21. impartial
'impartial' makes sense here — 'unbiased' and 'impartial' both mean 'neutral'.

22. declared
'declared' makes sense here — 'asserted' and 'declared' both mean 'insisted'.

23. impoverished
'impoverished' makes sense here — 'penniless' and 'impoverished' both mean 'poor'.

24. enthralled
'enthralled' makes sense here — 'fascinated' and 'enthralled' both mean 'captivated'.

25. complicated
'complicated' makes sense here — 'convoluted' and 'complicated' both mean 'complex'.

Test 24 — pages 74-76

1. foundation
Both words mean 'a support'.

2. build
Both words mean 'to increase'.

3. speed
Both words mean 'the pace of travel'.

4. attainable
Both words mean 'achievable'.

5. hint
Both words mean 'suggest'.

6. dainty
Both words mean 'delicate'.

7. harrowing
'harrowing' means 'very upsetting'.

8. peeve
'peeve' means 'a small irritation'.

9. etiquette
'etiquette' means 'polite behaviour'.

10. pant
'pant' means 'to breathe heavily'.

11. gallant
'gallant' means 'very courageous'.

12. facility
'facility' means 'a lack of difficulty'.

13. sparse
'copious' means 'plentiful', whereas 'sparse' means 'scarce'.

14. occupy
'vacate' means 'leave empty', whereas 'occupy' means 'live in'.

15. opaque
'transparent' means 'see-through', whereas 'opaque' means 'not see-through'.

16. meaningful
'petty' means 'trivial', whereas 'meaningful' means 'important'.

17. perish
'survive' means 'live', whereas 'perish' means 'die'.

18. wearily
'energetically' means 'actively', whereas 'wearily' means 'in a tired way'.

19. ab**ence**
'presence' means 'being in attendance', whereas 'absence' means 'being away'.

20. ILL
The complete word is FRILLS.

21. EBB
The complete word is WEBBED.

22. KIN
The complete word is BARKING.

23. ANT
The complete word is CHANTS.

24. ASK
The complete word is BASKETS.

25. ORE
The complete word is ADORES.

Test 25 — pages 77-78

1. **mole**
'mole' can mean 'an undercover agent' or 'a skin blemish'.

2. **compact**
'compact' can mean 'tightly packed together' or 'to press down and make smaller'.

3. **burrow**
'burrow' can mean 'a hole dug by an animal' or 'to dig a hole'.

4. **convict**
'convict' can mean 'someone found guilty of a crime' or 'to find someone guilty'.

5. **use**
'use' can mean 'the purpose of something' or 'to work with'.

6. su**ppr**ess
Both words mean 'to restrain'.

7. ven**d**etta
Both words mean 'hostility'.

8. **eerie**
Both words mean 'strange'.

9. am**usem**ent
Both words mean 'the feeling or expression of mirth'.

10. mono**tony**
Both words mean 'boredom'.

11. **discourtesy**
'politeness' means 'good manners', whereas 'discourtesy' means 'disrespect'.

12. **suddenly**
'gradually' means 'slowly', whereas 'suddenly' means 'all at once'.

13. **objection**
'approval' means 'permission', whereas 'objection' means 'disapproval'.

14. **humane**
'cruel' means 'heartless', whereas 'humane' means 'kind'.

15. **disperse**
'gather' can mean 'collect', whereas 'disperse' means 'scatter'.

16. **arduously**
'effortlessly' means 'easily', whereas 'arduously' means 'with difficulty'.

17. **gaudy**
'tasteful' means 'refined', whereas 'gaudy' means 'flashy'.

18. **obscure**
'reveal' means 'uncover', whereas 'obscure' means 'conceal'.

19. **awkward**
'convenient' means 'handy', whereas 'awkward' means 'inconvenient'.

20. **restraint**
'indiscipline' means 'misbehaviour', whereas 'restraint' means 'self-control'.

21. **black**
'ebony' is a shade of 'black' — it is a colour.

22. **disturbance**
A 'riot' is a 'disturbance' — it is an interruption of the peace.

23. **rank**
A 'sergeant' is a 'rank' — it is a type of army or police officer.

24. **tooth**
A 'molar' is a 'tooth' — it is used for grinding.

25. **fight**
A 'scuffle' is a 'fight' — it is a confused fight.

Puzzles 9 — page 79

Word Builder

be**drag**gled en**rich**ing dis**heart**ened at**tuned**

Sign Spellings

considerate pa**s**sengers
m**i**scellaneous pr**e**cious
Medite**r**ranean Medley
The missing letters spell out the word **cosier**.

Answers

Test 26 — pages 80-82

1. AIR
The complete word is FAIRER.

2. INK
The complete word is BLINKS.

3. SUM
The complete word is CONSUME.

4. RAY
The complete word is PRAYER.

5. ALE
The complete word is SEALED.

6. RAG
The complete word is ENRAGED.

7. saleable
The other three mean 'high-priced'.

8. sit
The other three are signs of respect.

9. consume
The other three mean 'a time when food is eaten'.

10. stench
The other three mean 'a pleasant smell'.

11. hesitantly
The other three mean 'without thought' or 'without planning'.

12. original
The other three are used to describe the state of food.

13. scorn
'admire' means 'to look up to', whereas 'scorn' means 'to look down on'.

14. faithful
'false' means 'disloyal', whereas 'faithful' means 'loyal'.

15. fulfilled
'disappointed' means 'not satisfied', whereas 'fulfilled' means 'satisfied'.

16. esteem
'disgrace' means 'being thought of badly', whereas 'esteem' means 'being thought of well'.

17. drought
'deluge' means 'flood', whereas 'drought' means 'lack of water'.

18. obvious
'subtle' means 'hard to observe', whereas 'obvious' means 'easily observed'.

19. pompous
Both words mean 'arrogant'.

20. adjust
Both words mean 'to alter'.

21. composure
Both words mean 'dignity'.

22. garments
Both words mean 'clothes'.

23. gratitude
Both words mean 'thanks'.

24. wonder
Both words mean 'to think about'.

25. critical
Both words mean 'needing immediate attention'.

Test 27 — pages 83-85

1. cellar
'cellar' makes sense here — it is the word that means 'basement', whereas 'seller' means 'a person who sells things'.

2. alter
'alter' makes sense here — it is the word that means 'to change', whereas 'altar' means 'a shrine'.

3. barren
'barren' makes sense here — it is the word that means 'infertile', whereas 'baron' is a type of nobleman.

4. fleas
'fleas' makes sense here — it is the word that means 'biting insects', whereas 'flees' means 'escapes'.

5. course
'course' makes sense here — it is the word that means 'route', whereas 'coarse' means 'harsh'.

6. jeans
'jeans' makes sense here — it is the word that means 'trousers', whereas 'genes' means 'DNA'.

7. highlight
'highlight' is the only correctly spelled word that can be made.

8. converse
'converse' is the only correctly spelled word that can be made.

9. moderate
'moderate' is the only correctly spelled word that can be made.

10. whereas
'whereas' is the only correctly spelled word that can be made.

11. wholesale
'wholesale' is the only correctly spelled word that can be made.

12. windswept
'windswept' is the only correctly spelled word that can be made.

13. motivate
'discourage' means 'deter', whereas 'motivate' means 'drive'.

14. assist
'impede' means 'to hinder', whereas 'assist' means 'to help'.

15. necessity
'luxury' means 'a nonessential item', whereas 'necessity' means 'something essential'.

16. freedom
'captivity' means 'imprisonment', whereas 'freedom' means 'not imprisoned'.

17. bland
'interesting' means 'fascinating', whereas 'bland' means 'dull'.

18. novice
'veteran' means 'expert', whereas 'novice' means 'beginner'.

19. infamous
'reputable' means 'well thought of', whereas 'infamous' means 'having a bad reputation'.

20. influential
'influential' makes sense here — 'powerful' and 'influential' both mean 'important'.

21. invigorating
'invigorating' makes sense here — 'exhilarating' and 'invigorating' both mean 'stimulating'.

22. exhaustion
'exhaustion' makes sense here — 'fatigue' and 'exhaustion' both mean 'tiredness'.

23. swiftly
'swiftly' makes sense here — 'promptly' and 'swiftly' both mean 'quickly'.

24. empty
'empty' makes sense here — 'devoid' and 'empty' both mean 'lacking'.

25. faltered
'faltered' makes sense here — 'hesitated' and 'faltered' both mean 'felt uncertain'.

Puzzles 10 — page 86

Bubble Trouble

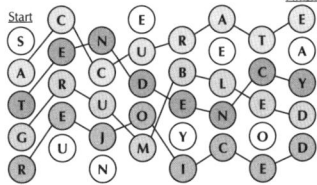

1. accurate   2. tendency   3. grumbled   4. rejoiced

Doughnut Words

1. calm   2. canal   3. amble   4. manual   5. ambulance

Test 28 — pages 87-89

1. dispute
A 'quarrel' is a 'dispute' — both words mean 'argument'.

2. award
A 'scholarship' is an 'award' — it is money given to help people study as a reward for high achievement.

3. icing
'fondant' is 'icing' — 'fondant' is used to decorate cakes.

4. seasoning
'pepper' is 'seasoning' — 'seasoning' is something that is used to flavour food.

5. appalling
'horrendous' and 'appalling' both mean 'terrible'.

6. epiphany
'revelation' and 'epiphany' both mean 'a realisation'.

7. flaunt
'parade' and 'flaunt' both mean 'to show off'.

8. coerce
'compel' and 'coerce' both mean 'to force'.

9. counterfeit
'fraudulent' and 'counterfeit' both mean 'fake'.

10. obligation
'commitment' and 'obligation' both mean 'a duty'.

11. fairly
'equitably' and 'fairly' both mean 'without favour to either side'.

12. enamoured
'infatuated' and 'enamoured' both mean 'to be in love'.

13. gathering
'congregation' and 'gathering' both mean 'a group'.

14. stubbornly
'doggedly' and 'stubbornly' both mean 'determinedly'.

15. ashen
'ashen' means 'very pale'.

16. gaffe
'gaffe' means 'a silly mistake'.

17. flail
'flail' means 'to swing wildly'.

18. absolution
'absolution' means 'freedom from guilt'.

19. frivolous
'frivolous' means 'not serious'.

20. fashionable
'outmoded' means 'unfashionable', whereas 'fashionable' means 'stylish'.

21. **deterrents**
'incentives' means 'motivations', whereas 'deterrents' means 'discouragements'.

22. **pliable**
'inflexible' means 'rigid', whereas 'pliable' means 'flexible'.

23. **disproved**
'validated' means 'confirmed', whereas 'disproved' means 'proved false'.

24. **vague**
'concrete' means 'solid', whereas 'vague' means 'uncertain'.

25. **diffidence**
'confidence' means 'self-belief', whereas 'diffidence' means 'shyness'.

Test 29 — pages 90-92

1. **book**
The other three refer to people who write.

2. **teenager**
The other three mean 'childish'.

3. **grocer**
The other three are places that sell prepared food.

4. **gallop**
The other three mean 'to jump forwards'.

5. **aspiration**
The other three mean 'boundary'.

6. **embarrass**
The other three mean 'obstruct'.

7. **house**
'house' can mean 'to provide space for' or 'a residence'.

8. **articulate**
'articulate' can mean 'able to speak well' or 'to express an idea clearly'.

9. **fall**
'fall' can mean 'to go down' or 'a defeat or downfall'.

10. **funny**
'funny' can mean 'strange' or 'amusing'.

11. **counter**
'counter' can mean 'to speak against' or 'a board game item'.

12. **recall**
'recall' can mean 'to provoke a memory' or 'a recollection'.

13. **des**ti**tute**
'affluent' means 'rich', whereas 'destitute' means 'poor'.

14. **wel**com**e**
'reject' means 'refuse', whereas 'welcome' means 'accept'.

15. **opt**ion**al**
'vital' means 'essential', whereas 'optional' means 'not essential'.

16. **dis**cord
'peace' means 'calm', whereas 'discord' means 'chaos'.

17. **dis**connect
'attach' means 'join', whereas 'disconnect' means 'break apart'.

18. **certa**in
'indefinite' means 'vague', whereas 'certain' means 'definite'.

19. **arr**iv**al**
'departure' means 'leaving a place', whereas 'arrival' means 'coming to a place'.

20. **considered**
'considered' makes sense here — 'contemplated' and 'considered' both mean 'thought about'.

21. **adversary**
'adversary' makes sense here — 'opponent' and 'adversary' both mean 'a rival'.

22. **fathom**
'fathom' makes sense here — 'comprehend' and 'fathom' both mean 'to understand'.

23. **eminent**
'eminent' makes sense here — 'distinguished' and 'eminent' both mean 'well-regarded'.

24. **exiled**
'exiled' makes sense here — 'banished' and 'exiled' both mean 'thrown out'.

25. **precarious**
'precarious' makes sense here — 'risky' and 'precarious' both mean 'dangerous'.

Puzzles 11 — page 93

Whose Dinosaur is Whose?
Mindy's dinosaur is **vicious** and **greedy** — it's **Ruby**.
Tamal's dinosaur is **irritable** and **feral** — it's **Ralph**.
Felicity's dinosaur is **curious** and **sociable** — it's **Rex**.

Test 30 — pages 94-96

1. USE
The complete word is REUSES.

2. ILL
The complete word is QUILLS.

3. OWL
The complete word is PROWLED.

4. ASK
The complete word is UNASKED.

5. OIL
The complete word is COILED.

6. AIM
The complete word is CLAIMED.

7. tail
'tail' makes sense here — it is the word that means 'rear', whereas 'tale' means 'story'.

8. whose
'whose' makes sense here — it is the word that means 'belonging to', whereas 'who's' means 'who is'.

9. rows
'rows' makes sense here — it is the word that means 'lines', whereas 'rose' is a flower.

10. minor
'minor' makes sense here — it is the word that means 'small', whereas 'miner' means 'person who works in a mine'.

11. bow
'bow' makes sense here — it is the word that means 'bending over', whereas 'bough' means 'a branch'.

12. manor
'manor' makes sense here — it is the word that means 'mansion', whereas 'manner' means 'behaviour'.

13. undermine
'empower' means 'give power to', whereas 'undermine' means 'weaken'.

14. demote
'elevate' means 'to make more important', whereas 'demote' means 'to make less important'.

15. disobedience
'compliance' means 'doing what you're told', whereas 'disobedience' means 'not doing what you're told'.

16. differ
'coincide' means 'to be in agreement', whereas 'differ' means 'to be dissimilar'.

17. compliment
'insult' means 'an abusive comment', whereas 'compliment' means 'a flattering comment'.

18. thoughtless
'discreet' means 'careful', whereas 'thoughtless' means 'inconsiderate'.

19. illusion
Both words mean 'something that isn't really there'.

20. tireless
Both words refer to someone or something that never tires.

21. infuriate
Both words mean 'to enrage'.

22. qualified
Both words mean 'capable'.

23. plunder
Both words mean 'to steal'.

24. pledge
Both words mean 'to promise'.

25. distort
Both words mean 'to twist the truth'.

Test 31 — pages 97-99

1. characteristic
Both words mean 'a character trait'.

2. tardy
Both words mean 'delayed'.

3. pragmatic
Both words mean 'sensible'.

4. fabricate
Both words mean 'to make up'.

5. eradicate
Both words mean 'to destroy'.

6. delusion
Both words mean 'a deception'.

7. overbear
'overbear' is the only correctly spelled word that can be made.

8. offspring
'offspring' is the only correctly spelled word that can be made.

9. milestone
'milestone' is the only correctly spelled word that can be made.

10. mainstream
'mainstream' is the only correctly spelled word that can be made.

11. hindsight
'hindsight' is the only correctly spelled word that can be made.

12. tailspin
'tailspin' is the only correctly spelled word that can be made.

13. mind
'mind' can mean 'to be concerned about' or 'to look after'.

14. experiment
'experiment' can mean 'to carry out a scientific investigation' or 'a scientific procedure'.

15. import
'import' can mean 'significance' or 'an item brought in from abroad'.

16. leg
'leg' can mean 'appendage' or 'a phase of something'.

17. just
'just' can mean 'no more than' or 'morally right'.

18. intrigue
'intrigue' can mean 'a scheme' or 'to arouse interest'.

19. cease
Both words mean 'to stop'.

20. brusque
Both words mean 'curt'.

21. client
Both words mean 'buyer'.

22. thorough
Both words mean 'complete'.

23. admonish
Both words mean 'to tell off'.

24. brazen
Both words mean 'unashamed'.

25. interval
Both words mean 'a pause'.

Puzzles 12 — page 100

Cross Words

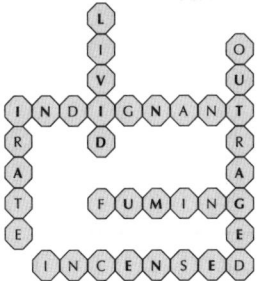

Bunch the Balloons

The complete words are **agreeable, disable, disagree, disagreeable, dismiss, remark, remarkable, regain, remiss, unable, unmissable, unremarkable**.

Progress Chart

Use this chart to keep track of your score for each test.

	Score		Score		Score
Test 1		Test 12		Test 23	
Test 2		Test 13		Test 24	
Test 3		Test 14		Test 25	
Test 4		Test 15		Test 26	
Test 5		Test 16		Test 27	
Test 6		Test 17		Test 28	
Test 7		Test 18		Test 29	
Test 8		Test 19		Test 30	
Test 9		Test 20		Test 31	
Test 10		Test 21			
Test 11		Test 22			

Look back at your scores once you've done all the tests. Each test is out of 25 marks. Work out which kind of mark you scored most often:

0-15 marks — Go back to basics and work on your question technique.

16-20 marks — You're nearly there — go back over the questions you found tricky.

21+ marks — You're a Vocabulary star.

Progress Chart